"How it is that animals understand thing[s...]
but it is certain that they do understand. Perhaps there is a soul
hidden in everything and it can always speak, without even
making a sound, to another soul." ~*Frances Hodgson Burnet*

As I was editing the stories featured in this book, I noticed how many times some words appear, especially "soul," "love," "bond" and "heart."

At first I thought it might be repetitious, but it became very clear that these words define the deep connection between you—altruistic, merciful humans—and your rescues...and vice versa.

Animals feel emotions like we do. They know when they have been saved. Their capacity to love is endless, their gratitude undeniable. And, just as we were there in their darkest hour, they are always there for ours.

This book is a love letter to those who so selflessly devote time, effort and loving care to all creatures, large and small. It is a testament to man's goodness and a tribute to the animals' loyalty.

>   ***My dream*** is that it will inspire more adoptions.
>
>   ***My wish*** is that it will promote animal welfare.
>
>   ***My hope*** is that it will help raise funds for shelters.
>
>   ***My thanks*** go to each of you for your acts of kindness and for sharing your amazing stories.

A special thank you also goes to my friend Tracy Burg for so generously contributing her time and her art direction talents.

This book is for all of you, with much love.

 Fifi

Brutality to an animal is cruelty to mankind— it is only the difference in the victim.

~Alphonse de Lamartine

RESCUE ME

Love Stories of Humans and the Animals They Saved

Published by Fifi Girl Media, Inc.
Sarasota, Florida

© Fifi O'Neill 2018. All rights reserved.

Library of Congress Control Number: 2018955340

ISBN 978-0- 692-17664 -1

Printed in the United States by Coastal Printing

Designer: Tracy Burg

Cover frame: ©iStock/Rangga-Wijaya; Paw prints: ©iStock/kimikodate; Paw heart shape: ©iStock/bulentgultek; Photo frame: ©iStock/Warmworld; Cat illustration: ©iStock/Tanyasun; Pink leash: ©iStock/Youngvet; Pet friends: ©iStock/FatCamera; Fifi's intro photo: by Elizabeth Kirkpatrick

ADOPT, DON'T SHOP!

SHOOTER

Shooter was rescued from an abusive situation. He was deathly afraid of men. If you called him, he would crawl to you on his belly then cringe if you reached for his head to pat him.

He is still shy with strangers, but sleeps right beside me in bed, usually on his back! He now *adores* my husband and my adult son. He is an all around *perfect* dog, great big brother to his sisters Pancho and Lefty (continuing the country music theme), although they show him who's in charge!

We also adopted Owen, a dog that could be his brother and Shooter is thrilled to have the power to tell him what to do!

Shooter was on Petfinder with his twin brother; he was called Socrates and his brother was Plato. We had to change his name for several reasons, but, trust me, a deep thinker he is not!

We *love* him so much, and can't say enough how important it is to *adopt*, not shop! ~**PAT** ♥

HOME SWEET HOME

ZOEY

SADIE

SADIE & ZOEY

Sadie was my first little rescue. She and her six siblings were found in a box behind a dumpster at around 5 weeks old. I was able to get all of her brothers and sister *adopted* through social media but Sadie was the smallest and I knew I had to keep her. She'll be 6 this year and hasn't slowed down yet.

We got **Zoey** about two months after Kyle and I got married. We had not intended to get a second dog at the time but her picture popped up on the local SPCA Facebook page and she had the biggest, saddest eyes. I then found out that there is actually a thing called "Little black dog syndrome" and, much like older dogs in shelters, little black dogs are really hard to get adopted as they are often looked over because their coats don't stand out in the dark kennels; they are sometime not even seen. After learning about LBDS I worried about her being put down because she had already been at the shelter for several months without much interest. The next day my husband and I went and adopted her. She is the *most loving puppy* and would rather be cuddled all day than chase a ball. She will be 3 this year. ~**AMANDA** ♥

DON'T LET ME SCARE YOU

MAYA

Pit bulls, like it or not, have a negative reputation but they can be *big pussycats!*

I used to rescue pit bulls, but after several years I decided I was not going to do this anymore because of the emotional trauma when they passed. But then I came across **Maya** at the Pasadena shelter... I have had her since that day.

When I first got her she was afraid of everything. She didn't even bark for the first year! Now, five years later, she runs our apartment and *loves her family*. And we love her! ~**ANDRE** ♥

When I first got her she was **afraid of everything.**

MEANT FOR EACH OTHER

ELI & RALPHIE

Many years ago, I was at a yard sale in the small rural area in Oregon where I lived. I saw a scruffy young dog running around and commented to the person in charge of the sale that the dog was *adorable*. The man was quick to respond: "If you like him, take him. If you don't, I'm going to take him out and shoot him this afternoon." I was shocked by his remark and grabbed the dog as quickly as I could.

The man shared that **Ralphie** was Airedale and Australian Shepard mix. I took him to the vet before I even took him home. He had some imbedded porcupine quills in his face that were infected and a larger infected gash on one of his legs. He was pretty smelly, too. We determined that he was about 9 months old. He got all of his neglected shots and an appointment to neuter him later was made. My yard sale find cost me close to $400 that day! But Ralphie fit in with the family like it was *meant to be*. He never did get over his attraction to porcupines and submitted to all of the quill removals without ever a growl. He has spent time with all of the kids in the town and has always been very protective of his family. He is the most even-tempered, *sweet dog* any one could be blessed with.

Fast forward to the present: Ralphie is turning 20 this year. I find this remarkable for an almost 100-pound dog. He is blind, stiff and can be cranky.

The young man with him in the picture is my son, Eli. He has autism and just turned 19. His most constant friend has always been Ralphie.

I wanted to share a story of *true love*, and the very best yard sale find ever in the history of the world. ~**DONNA** ♥

LOVED & MISSED

TIGER & THUMPER

This is my **Tiger** and his buddy, **Thumper**. I also had Tiger's brother, Blue, and my Godmother had his sister, Emily.

Over 20 years ago, I rescued three kittens from under an abandoned house by the river. I kept two, Tiger and Blue, and my Godmother took the other.

Unfortunately, Blue died several years ago.

Recently, I had to make the gut-wrenching decision to say goodbye to my beloved Tiger. He was my companion for almost half of my life and he was very *loved* and will be so missed!

RIP my sweet, sweet boy. ~**ANGELA** ♥

WITH AN OPEN HEART

SADIE BLUE

This is my **Sadie Blue**. I gave her that name because I was sad and blue when I got her.

My former dog died unexpectedly at 10 years old. She had been my first fur *baby* as an adult.

But, I opened my *heart* again and adopted a sweet, fuzzy puppy that is now almost 100 pounds—just don't tell her that! ~**CAYCE** ♥

THE RIGHT CHOICE

MOLLY

Having recently bought a farm, I thought it was it was time to embrace country life and add a dog to our family. It was something I felt deeply in my soul, but the question was: which dog would be the best dog for our family? Since I have a non-verbal daughter with special needs, I began to research dogs that might help me keep an eye on her. A Collie seemed to be the answer. As I perused the Texas Collie Rescue website, I saw a 2-year-old girl wearing a pink cast. She was *beautiful* and I felt so drawn to her. I showed her to my girls, Elise and Evie, and my husband, Kevin, as we thought about how she might become a part of our family.

I went to buy fabric for Evie's school project and passed a lady wearing a Collie-print shirt. It was not something I had ever seen before. Was it a sign? I stopped and asked her about it. She said that she ran the Texas Collie Rescue group. I couldn't believe it! I told her that I had been admiring **Molly** online. I asked if she was still available and if I could see her. As it turned out, Molly was at the groomer near our house, so I popped in to meet her. My *heart* melted. She had such a gentle and sweet spirit.

I asked to come visit her again the next day. She was so adorable; I knew she was the one. They said she wasn't ready for adoption because her leg hadn't finished healing (she had been hit by

She was so **adorable**; I knew she was the one.

a car and her shoulder had been dislocated). The previous owner could not afford the vet bills and had relinquished ownership to the Texas Collie Rescue after the accident. I found out later the other reason why she was "not ready for adoption"—they were very attached to her. She was one of their favorites due to her very affectionate nature.

I turned in an application to adopt Molly. I visited her several more times in an attempt to prove what a good mom I would be. One day, my daughter Evie came with me for a visit. I was a little concerned because she was afraid of dogs. They asked her if she liked Molly and then I thought about what a mistake I had made bringing her with me. Of course you can imagine Evie's answer: A big, fat "No!" Still, I knew that wasn't really the truth, but I also knew that would change once we actually had a dog. I figured they would bond in about a week. But how was I going to convince the rescue group that she would actually come around? Things had taken a turn for the worse.

The next day I got word from the rescue group. We had been turned down for adoption. I asked why, but I knew the answer. They couldn't send Molly somewhere she wasn't *loved*. Molly would know that Evie didn't like her. Dogs sense these things. I pointed out that Molly would be my dog and that I loved her already. My plea fell on deaf ears. They politely said no. But the next day they called back and said that they had a *change of heart*. They would allow us to adopt as long as she was my dog. And we also had to promise she would be an indoor dog. Of course I had no problem with this rule. Then they added another stipulation that was not on their form: She had to sleep in our room with us. I could tell they were struggling with the idea of letting her go. But we agreed to the terms. Then, there was the home visit we had to pass. They brought Molly to our house a few days later, inspecting the yard, the fence and everything in the house. We passed. She was ours! Evie was still keeping her distance but I felt confident the frost would thaw with time, but even I was shocked by what actually happened. Molly was so *adorable* that she had Evie eating out of her paw within 24 hours. She may have started out as my dog, but she quickly became Evie's.

True confession: Molly only slept in our room for a few nights. After that, Evie insisted that Molly sleep with her. They have remained best friends for life. **~ANITA** ♥

ONE LUCKY DAY

CRICKET

We stopped at PetSmart on a Saturday to get food for my son's frog. As we turned around to leave, we noticed that the animal shelter from which we always had gotten our previous dogs was having an adoption fair.

It was then that we saw her—the little brindle dog in the top cage, looking scared. They asked us if we wanted to hold her and we never put her back down.

After a week of writing down names on a list for this little stray from Chicago, our family decided to name her **Cricket**!

She is an Italian Greyhound mix with a *big personality* in a little package! She adjusted to our family, as well as to our calico cat, Lily, and our other dog, Dixie, in a heartbeat. She is well behaved, spins around like a little cyclone and throws her toys to us!

We always tell her she has found her people and she is such a *happy* dog now! ~**LYNN** ♥

They asked us if we wanted to hold her
and **we never put her back down.**

IN THE NICK OF TIME

TIGER

Tiger is a 4-year-old Maine coon mix. He was rescued from a kill shelter in Dalton, Georgia. We saw his picture on the Internet and we wanted him but we were out of town at the time. Fridays are kill days at that shelter and any pet that doesn't get adopted through the week gets euthanized.

We called our friend in Georgia (we lived in Chattanooga at the time) and she, along with her kids, went to the shelter and *rescued* him on Thursday afternoon. If she hadn't gone, he would have been killed that following morning. So we saved him just in the nick of time. We couldn't imagine our lives without our baby Tiger. He brings us so much *joy!*

KROGER

Kroger is our new baby. He is 8 months old. His name has a lot to do with his rescue story. Our church was hosting a fall festival and my friend asked me to make a

run to a nearby Kroger grocery store to get some chips. As we walked to the car, a kitten came running out from under a car and started meowing. He was so scared and so *sweet*. I grabbed him and put him in my friend's car. When I got back to the church, I got the kids to help get him in a box in my car and drove home.

He stayed in our garage for two days with a warm bed and food. Then we took him to our local Humane Society. When we got there, the girl at the counter scanned him and he was chipped. They contacted his owner and told them that we had found their *kitty*. The owner said that she had adopted him but she didn't want him anymore. She had actually given him up to her daughter who also didn't want him so she threw him on the street! I couldn't believe a person could be so heartless towards a loving creature. We took him home and he has been part of our family since. We completely *adore him* and we are grateful he chose us to be his forever home. **~ANA** ♥

THREE OF A KIND

RHONDA & DIABLO

DIABLO, DIOS & HURLEY

Diablo has always been an *old soul*, ever since the day, in 2004, when his dad picked him out of a group of his brothers and sisters who were in a tin-roofed building behind a police station in Florida. This building had no walls, only chicken wire, and basically served as "the pound." While his siblings were jumping about, Diablo was sleeping in the corner alone. Justin named him Diablo, which has always been a joke, because he is (and was) the furthest thing from a devil, but his reddish coat lent itself well to the name, I suppose. Little did Diablo know he would end up in a military family and be a well-traveled dog, living in several states over the next 14 years. He gained a younger brother and best friend, **Dios**, and then, years later, another brother, Gator.

Throughout his years, Diablo hasn't been one to romp around, play fetch or anything else dog-like. He is content just walking around, doing his own thing. His *favorite things* to do are to lie in a sunny patch of grass and to dote on the "stuffy" collection he has amassed over the years. He is very meticulous in their care, and has had some of the same toys for over 12 years now. He has his favorites and will line them up in a row, and sometimes—if they're lucky—they get to go to the sunny patch of grass with him.

Diablo's movements now match the old soul that he has always been. We learned a little over a year ago that he suffers from degenerative myelopathy, which is comparable to ALS in humans. His disease is terminal. We are hoping for an early spring here in New Hampshire, so he can enjoy his sunny patch again before traveling to the Rainbow Bridge.

We adopted **Dios** in the summer of 2015 from the folks at Oklahoma City Animal Welfare. We went in that day with the intention of finding a brother for Diablo.

We walked several corridors of kennels, each lined with sad faces, begging to come home with us. Near the end of our visit, we found the most hyper, *excited* pup named Dallas (approximately 6-8 months old) who seemed to have springs in his feet. He could jump to the moon if he tried. We knew he was the one. As we walked him out to the car, he hurriedly tugged at his leash with a big grin, ready to go home.

He met his fur-brother, Diablo, and they were instantly *best buddies*. We renamed him "Dios" as a sort of play off of his brother's name. The story that came with little Dios was that his family moved and couldn't (or wouldn't) take him with them. What they lost, we gained. I had no idea that

DIOS

this little boy would be my shadow, literally one step behind me wherever I went, for the next 12+ years.

If your heart could survive outside your body, he was mine. I say, "was" because he passed a short while ago. Writing this is difficult for me but it is my way to honor him and the special connection we shared.

Facebook saved **Hurley**'s life. He had spent several of his first few months in a kill shelter in the panhandle of Florida, where we were living at the time. He had *won the hearts* of staff members, which bought him some time. But as Hurley (aka Gator) got older and there was no interested potential adopter, he was put on "the list." His date fell on Friday the 13th. The shelter staff begged for at least the weekend to find him a home, at which time, they plastered Facebook with his photo in *hopes* that someone would save him. Once your name is on "the list," only a rescue can pull you out of the shelter. Long story short, his photo found its way to us by means of several shares and re-posts. We connected with the shelter and the rescue to secure his freedom on that Monday, which was to be his last day. Hurley came to live with his two new fur-brothers, Diablo and Dios. This headstrong, stubborn boy made life difficult at times but he was the *best snuggler* in the entire world. He lived for games of throwing a ball, frisbee, sticks and basically anything else he could catch in his monstrous mouth...which, by the way, is how he earned his new name, "Gator." We have millions of photos of Gator, but this one is the most poignant. You see, Gator was only 6 years old in 2016 when a mast cell tumor was found on his leg. We had it removed, but, during his surgery, it was discovered that he also had cancer in his mouth. This photo was taken 5 minutes before the doggy oncologist basically told us that there was nothing we could do for our *sweet boy*. I look back at this photo and it reminds me of the hope we had, going into that appointment.

Diablo, Dios and Gator have been and will always remain in our *hearts*. We loved them dearly and always will. ~**RHONDA** ♥

He could **jump to the moon** if he tried.

JUSTIN & HURLEY

ALMOST TRIPLETS

LEMMY, LUCY & MINNIE

As soon as we moved into our home we knew that we wanted to *adopt* a kitten from an animal shelter. We both came from homes with three or more pets and our new home was just too quiet. So we started our search for a kitten.

We eventually came across two 4-month old kittens, a boy and a girl, who were brother and sister and were up for adoption. We decided to put in our application to adopt both of them. There was also a 5-month old calico cat with them.

When our application was approved, we went back to get our two kittens and it was then we decided to not split up this darling kitty trio. So we adopted all three that night! The boy is now named **Lemmy**, the black little girl cat is **Lucille**, aka "Lucy," and the black-and-white calico is named **Minerva**, aka "Minnie."

They are adjusting to their new home quite nicely and we *love* having all three of them running around and *playing*! There is never a dull moment around here now! ~**KAYLYN & CARTER** ♥

FROM MISTREATED TO MUCH LOVED

LUCKY JACK

Lucky Jack is a purebred Standard Parti-poodle. We discovered him sitting in a crate inside a windowless garage warehouse. He was 10 months old. The crate was too small for him. He had never been trimmed, brushed or bathed and was covered in his own filth. His eyes were actually matted shut.

We owned the warehouse and were appalled to see his condition. We called his owner and asked her to come over right away. This woman had been raising shih tzus in her home and we were aware that she had received citations for trying to sell puppies for cash. Her puppies were inbred and very unhealthy. She acquired Lucky (then named Boston) with plans to raise Labradoodles. She could not keep Lucky at her rented home because of his size so he was kept in this garage.

When she arrived, my husband, Bob, said, "Give me this dog or I am calling the police." She replied that he couldn't have it. "That's a $1500 dog!" she said. Bob repeated that she should turn over the dog or he would call the police. Because of her past legal problems with dogs, she told Bob to take him but then added, "You can't have his papers, and I just want you to know he is in this crate because he is too wild." She also told us that his leg had been broken when he was younger, and he had a pin in his femur. We found out later that her son broke Lucky's leg!

We brought Lucky home that afternoon. I tried to wash him, but his coat was so matted and filthy it was impossible. I called a groomer to come to our house. When she looked at him, I could tell that she was considering calling the police, too! I explained the situation to her and she got to work. It took over three hours to clean him up, and, beneath his coat, he was literally a bag of bones.

Next step was to see the vet. Lucky had a terrible infection in his digestive system and his leg. Slowly but surely, his health improved.

He has been sleeping in our bedroom since his first day, and his behavior has always been that of a perfect gentleman. Lucky is now nearly 13 years old. He comes to my acupuncture office every day and is the most popular "person" there! Other than his limp, which has never gone away, he is in perfect health and is *adored* by hundreds! ~**DANEE** ♥

MASTER OF HIS DOMAIN

HENRY

I can't believe it's been six years since **Henry** came into our lives! My husband and I filled out an application with Golden Retriever Rescue, Education, and Training, an organization that rescues and provides foster care and placement for Golden Retrievers in our area. We met a year-and-a-half-old Golden who *stole my heart*, but her foster parents chose somewhere else for her forever home.

Then we saw a description of Henry online, and my husband fell in *love*—although I was skeptical. He was only nine months old, and his fosters described him as an "old soul," less rambunctious and more serious than most Goldens his age. He had strange gold eyes, and his serious nature seemed standoffish to me. But my husband wanted him, and I figured if he liked him so much, he'd play a really active role in taking care of the dog, so we agreed to take him.

Henry jumped in the car with us and never looked back. Neither have I! His gold eyes soon turned brown, except in bright sunlight, and, as he grew accustomed to his new surroundings, his "standoffishness" disappeared. He *loves* having his belly scratched, cuddling with us, and sitting at the highest point in our yard observing the plants, trees, squirrels, and birds—master of his domain! He is still a little shy with strangers, and often greets them with his largest chew bone, as if to say, "See this? This is mine! What do you have?" Offer him a treat, though, and he's your friend for life. Henry's "old soul" has gotten progressively younger through the years, and he gets more and more *playful* all the time, while still remembering the lessons he learned in obedience school.

Henry works as a comfort dog at our local university to relieve stress during finals and will soon start visiting two assisted living facilities to bring *cheer* to the residents. We're so glad he rescued us. ~**BARBARA** ♥

LIFE SAVER

LILLY ROSE

I found three pups in a shoe box in the back alley behind a local shopping center. **Lilly Rose** was the only one who survived.

I feel very *blessed* to have saved her life.

Now I am feeling fortunate she is being so *loving* to me while life changes are now happening to us both. ~**LISA** ♥

TENDER MERCY

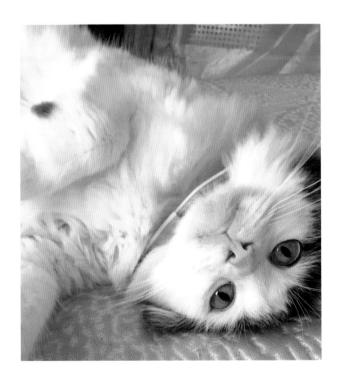

GRACIE

This is **Grace** (Gracie). I rescued her from a shelter where she lived in a cage for the first six months of her life.

She could not walk, jump or run and had no social skills. With lots of *love* and *patience* she is now well, loves her mama and surroundings.

She has a little *heart* shape on one of her paws (she reminds me of Duchess and Marie from Disney's Aristocats).

She is the most loving—and lovable—cat I have ever had! ~**PAULINA** ♥

LEARNING TO LOVE

TRAGEN

I have always been a large dog breed lover. I was raised with boxers all my life. As for pit bulls, I had heard the stories of the breed being aggressive. I was introduced to two pit bulls that loved to play at the park, be lazy, and *adored* their owner. When I decided I wanted to rescue a dog, I had my mind set on rescuing a pit bull in Austin, Texas. I did my research online and had ten pit bulls to choose from at the shelter. While all of the dogs were great, I did not connect with any of them.

I believe that, in many ways, the dog chooses you. I walked around the shelter and saw a red nose sitting in the corner, alone and silent. He had just been fixed and was very swollen and deformed. He also had many cuts and scars on him from seemingly violent environments (what I presumed to be fighting rings). There was no guarantee he would heal. People who saw him walked by quickly making disgusted faces because he was so swollen. I could tell he could feel it.

After many passes, I made the decision to go in his kennel and meet him. He perked up right away. We talked a little bit. I asked if he wanted to go take a walk. He got right up and stuck to my side. He was very sore and did not play much but I made the decision that Tragen was coming home with me. When I got him in the car I could see he was so *happy*. He obviously had never witnessed a soft touch or heard a soft voice. I let him sleep the rest of the day.

That evening my friend brought over his dog. Unfortunately Tragen ran after my friend's boxer and attacked him. I could see he had been trained to do this. No one was hurt but it was pretty terrifying. A few days passed and Tragen had become *comfortable* and calm with his current living situation. He began to heal from his procedure. Once again, we tried to have dog friends over, but he did the same thing. I felt that I had made a mistake. I realize today, though, that I was not being a good leader to Tragen and helping him understand what was expected of him. I will be the first to say the breed is not for everyone and they need order and leadership—an alpha.

I looked Tragen in the eyes and slapped him on the nose. I knew I had to make him understand that aggression would not be tolerated in my household and if he wanted to stay he would need to change. It was the craziest thing. Tragen put his head down, sat down then rolled over on his back and made a few crying noises. From that point on he always looked to me for direction. He is *friendly* with even the most fragile dogs and is now known as the nicest and friendliest dog at the shop where I work out. He is always willing to cuddle for hours and feels emotion at any level with a desire to try to make you feel better.

Tragen has become an ambassador of his breed. At the park, he plays fetch and *loves* to swim. He greets all dog friends with a kind lick to the face. He sits outside with me in the front yard while we do yard work. I believe Tragen made a decision to leave his past behind and become the best dog he knew he wanted to be. I believe dogs know when they have been rescued. I truly believe that. I was *lucky*. I found Tragen, and Tragen found me. ~**BEAR** ♥

TINY FRIENDS WITH BIG IMPACT

LU LU

Last year, my oldest daughter was diagnosed with breast cancer. My granddaughter, Blakelee, didn't quite understand everything that was going on and became withdrawn. One day, on a trip to the pet store, she found a guinea pig, **Lu Lu**, and they quickly became *friends*. Lu Lu went everywhere with her! She helped Blakelee get through a very tough year. I could hear her at night talking to Lu Lu and telling her secrets. We all love Lu Lu!

Blakelee was so taken by her little confidant and *loved* her so much she asked for a second guinea pig. So back to the pet store we went. She named her new friend Emma. Apparently no one knew Emma was expecting! So now Blakeley has 4 little friends! She *loves* them all and so do we! There is no doubt that animals often rescue us instead of the other way around. ~**LISA** ♥

HUNGRY NO MORE

PARIS

This is my little rescue, **Paris**. My daughter is a groomer. One day a man brought in Paris and said she belonged to an elderly woman near him. Paris was malnourished and in terrible shape. My daughter groomed the poor little girl. The salon owner and my daughter bought food and gave it to the man and told him that if they could not care for her to bring her back and they would find her a *home*. He dumped her off a few days later.

My daughter knew I wanted a small rescue. She called me to come by the salon and of course I went right over. Because Paris was 4 years old I kept her name the same. She is a mix of Chihuahua and Maltese. She is the *sweetest* ever. She was in such poor shape! I had to vacuum constantly because she wanted to eat anything she found on the floor. After a few months she learned to eat from a dish. She has stolen our *hearts!* ~**BELINDA** ♥

She is a mix of Chihuahua and Maltese.
She is the sweetest ever.

MOVING IN

TIGGER & THE OUTIES

My boy **Tigger** wanted me to share his story and photo. We sure love our little boy! ~**JOYA** ♥

My name is Thomas J. Schmiggens, but my mom and dad call me Tigger. I was just a little boy when I met my dad for the first time. I was an "outie"—that's what we kitty kids who lived outside called each other. I lived under a big bush with my pals Sydney, a big black-and-white tuxedo cat, and Hosta, a gray-and-white tuxedo cat who liked to hang out under a hosta plant and meow at the people passing by. Sydney and Hosta were real outies. They had always lived on the street and they were *pretty smart*. I was a "throwaway." I guess my original family only wanted a kitten, so when I started to get big, they sent me packing.

Anyhow, I met my human dad on the porch one day. He was *really nice*. He and my human mom set up a nice house for us on the porch and fed us every day. We had a soft thing to sleep on (now I know it's called a blanket) and it was nice to move out from under the bush. And we had plenty of food, except when the raccoons tried to get it. But we were smart—we learned to get to the bowl first and gobble it all up.

I soon learned about this thing called "*treats*." They come from a bag that makes the best sound! When I heard that sound, I would come running! Yummmmmm! TREATS! I still love the sound of treats!

One day, I felt a chill in the air. I didn't like that. The wind was blowing and wet stuff was hitting my nose. I jumped up on a big thing (later on I learned it was called a chair) on the porch and meowed. My dad (well, he wasn't my dad yet) came out to see who was making so much noise. I was a loud little boy. He said something about rain and scooped me up and took me inside the house. I was scared! He kept petting me and talking to me about something called a storm. I wasn't sure what that meant, but I was *happy* the wet stuff wasn't hitting my nose any more. And I found a new friend, a boy named Fluffkin who was bigger than me, but he seemed okay and he showed me where the food was.

That's the day I became an "innie." I missed my outie friends, Sydney and Hosta, but they came to visit every day and we got to play through the window. And I had a new dad and a new mom and a big brother named Fluffkin. That was seven years ago, the day I rescued my humans.

Sincerely,

Tigger Lord (*aka Thomas J. Scmiggens*)

THERE'S ALWAYS ROOM FOR ONE MORE

SQUEAKER

SQUEAKER

When I saw this short-legged dog running full speed down railroad tracks along a busy six-lane road, I couldn't drive by without trying to help. That was 12 years ago.

We already had quite a **menagerie...**

DUNE

Dune was found wandering the streets of East Dallas by a friend of my husband's who had seen a "Free Puppy" sign in a yard.

My husband stepped up and brought him home. He called me first and asked if I was okay with that. I said sure, knowing that a "Free Puppy" sign was not typically in the best interest of the dog, and thinking I would be able to find him a good home. We already had quite a menagerie...two dogs, two parrots, a turtle, a bunny and a horse.

Well things didn't turn out that way... As the saying goes: There's always room for one more!

DUNE

I also do cottontail rehabilitation with Texas Metro Wildlife. The bunny with the ice bottle could not be released due to a trauma that caused a neurological condition called "head tilt." He has been with me for two years now.

Although I do my best to keep them wild (no cuddles, no pets) providing the bunnies with a food source has won their *trust*.

Another cute little fellow shows up every day about feeding time. You can learn more about cottontail bunny rehabilitation or about Texas Metro Wildlife at *txmetrowildlife.org* or search "wildlife rescue" to locate ones in your state. **~DONNA** ♥

HOME & SAFE

WEEZIE

HUDSON

GOLDIE

MADDIE

HUDSON, MADDIE, GOLDIE & WEEZIE

Hudson was adopted two years ago and is now a New York City dog. When he arrived, he was fearful of men and had, and still has, some issues walking the noisy streets of NYC. But he is much better and has made friends with men and enjoys his walks and heading to the dog park. He lives with my daughter, Jaime, and **Maddie** the cat.

Maddie was adopted from St. Hubert's Animal Welfare Center in Madison, New Jersey. She is a city kitty and *loves* to watch the happenings in the bustling streets from her spot near the window on the 29th floor. She loves the dahlias that I bring her in season from the garden but has been known to nibble on the petals.

Goldie was adopted by my dear friend Nancy and was the absolute *best* girl.

Weezie was a rescue that came with her name and yes she was a bit weezie! She is a *sweet* girl who wasn't wanted and was chained outside most of her days. Nancy and her family brought this beautiful girl into their home and lives. ~**CAROL** ♥

MISTAKEN IDENTITY

HANK

Hank is a girl, and was a feral that found her way into our yard in the Houston area in 2014 when she was approximately 6-7 months old. I spent many hours sitting on the patio while tossing food to her trying to get her to not be afraid of us, as she took off every time we stepped outside.

After a couple of months of feeding her and slowly working her inside the doorway, she made it inside...and never left. We named her Hank while she was still living outside, although the vet revealed to us that Hank was in fact a female; we decided the name would stay. Hank is still very skittish and won't let anyone pet her except me, but will sniff my husband's hand once in awhile.

Hank spends her days inside *sleeping* and chirping at the birds on the back deck. She is *loved* by my family and me. ~**CARI** ♥

THOUGHTFUL DECISION

CARLOS

One morning I was getting ready to go to a citywide yard sale with my friend in the Victorian town of Ferndale, California. I was waiting for her to arrive at my house when she texted me saying that her friend (who I hadn't met yet) would be joining us. When they arrived at my house, her friend had a little dog in a crate in her car. She started to explain why she had the dog with her. "We

had to evict the tenant at our rental property and she left behind her *puppy*, a 7-month-old pug/Chihuahua mix. I don't like dogs, but I don't know what to do with him and I don't want to take him to the shelter."

I suggested to leave the dog with my husband and our other *rescue*, a French bulldog. I thought he would get along (with the dog, not my husband). She told us his name was Carlos. My husband kindly agreed and off we went to find antique treasures in Ferndale. When we came back home and my friend went to get the puppy to put it in his crate, my husband said very matter-of-factly: "We'll keep him."

Now, I am a realist. We already had plenty of animals and one had recently passed away from old age, which I was still getting over. All the thoughts came into my head at once: We don't know anything about this dog. Is he potty trained? Does he bark all the time? Does he bite?

He was incredibly *cute* but taking in an animal is a huge responsibility. We all came to the conclusion that we would take Carlos on a two-week trial period to see how he would fit in with our family and our other pets. It was around day three of the trial period that I called my new friend and told her, "We will keep him!"

We can't imagine life without Carlos. He makes us smile every minute of every day. One of my daughters suffers from depression and Carlos was literally a *lifesaver*. He sleeps with her at night and he calms her during the tough times.

Sometimes things come together without trying too hard and that's when I know they were meant to be. We weren't looking for another pet. Carlos came to us because he was destined to be with our family. We celebrate his birthday on Valentine's Day and he is now 1 year old. ~**TANYA** ♥

HOPE, PURPOSE & REWARDS

PRINCE CHARMING & CINDERELLA

I wanted to share a picture of my daughter, Madison, with her two rescue horses. **Charming** (short for Prince Charming), the brown horse, was seized by the Humane Society after he was found being starved and left in a field to die. **Ella** (for Cinderella), the white one, was found by a friend of ours. She was in a dirt pen and was standing on her back legs trying to eat bark off trees to survive. Both were sick, emaciated and skittish around people.

My daughter had recently been diagnosed with rheumatoid arthritis at 19, and was facing an unknown future. These horses gave her a reason, a *purpose*. She is now studying psychology in college with the hopes of using these horses in therapy for troubled kids or soldiers with PTSD and other challenges. Madison did not just save these horses; I like to think they saved each other! ~**ASHLEY** ♥

Madison did not just save these horses;
I like to think **they saved each other**!

THREE AMIGOS

OLIVER, DARTAGNAN & NUTMEG

NUTMEG

Our **Oliver** is the big, fluffy, orange kitty. A friend of mine found him on the side of the road. She was driving along a back road and saw a tiny little thing. She thought it was a baby bunny. She stopped and discovered it was a kitten. No houses were around so she knew he was an orphan. She took him home and proceeded to ask around for a forever home for him. When we went to pick him up to provide that home, he was so teeny; he could fit in the palm of our hand. He was only 6 weeks old. We named him Oliver after Oliver Twist (another orphan). That was 5 years ago.

OLIVER

Our big white-and-tan boy is named **Dartagnan**, after one of The Three Musketeers (our kids named all of our kitties). Another friend had a kitty that got out of their house a week before she was scheduled to be spayed. Needless to say, the surgery had to be postponed because she ended up pregnant and had a litter of *kittens*. I remember sitting in the middle of the floor at her house, kittens all over the room. This tiny little fur ball was the only one that came over to me right away and curled up on my lap. He came home with us to join Oliver. That was 3 years ago.

Our little calico is **Nutmeg**. She is the baby who is looking in the mirror and on the arm of the rocking chair with Dartagnan. This past Christmas, another friend found a litter of kittens that been abandoned in their back barn...no mother to be found. All of the kittens, except Nutmeg, had frozen to death. So horrible! She tried to bring her into the house but the kitty would have no part of it! Poor Nutmeg was kept in their garage for a few days until she showed me a video of her. I saw this little gem and instantly fell in love. They brought her to our house that afternoon. She was a tiny little ball of *love*. When I took her to the vet the following week, I discovered she was only 5 weeks old. She has been such a little *joy*. Both Oliver and Dartagnan accepted her right away, but especially Dartagnan. He grooms her, *plays* with her and they have a big cat bed they both fit into for naps.

I carry the name Crazy Cat Lady with pride. ~**TRACEY** ♥

DARTAGNAN & NUTMEG

TWO PEAS IN A POD

We just have to say the word **"camp"** and they both go crazy barking...

LAVERNE & SHIRLEY

LAVERNE & SHIRLEY

These girls have stolen the *hearts* of many, one beat at a time. Our diva Chihuahua was adopted at 4 months old. She will be 11 this year. Her name was going to be Jellybean, but it just didn't fit her personality. She was a pup that did not like to get dirty and loved the sunshine, so **Laverne** was more fitting.

She was crate-trained, until mummy went to London for work for a week and came home to find her sleeping in bed with daddy. No crate needed after that; Laverne *loves* her daddy.

A year later, we rescued a 1-year-old Chorkie (Chihuahua and Yorkshire terrier mix). The first day they met they were two peas in a pod. Laverne had found her **Shirley**!

Shirley is a quirky girl and *loves* to be outside in her yard playing with the squirrels or jumping in the snow—she is our little snow fox. Having high anxiety, she wears her ThunderShirt during fireworks or stressful storms. She sure has a tender *heart*, too.

They both love to camp in the summers here in Michigan. We just have to say the word *"camp"* and they both go crazy barking, saying let's go on an adventure.

They have a lot of Facebook friends that are dear to us. One in particular is Robbee from Australia. Laverne has been his girl for 9 years. Now that is true *puppy love*. ~**LAURA** ♥

IN THE NAME OF LOVE

MURPHY

GRACIE & MURPHY

Murphy is an "*old soul*" boy who we rescued almost eight years ago. He sings and loves nothing better than to cuddle up next to you and talk! He's believed to be an Airedale/German shepherd cross who has a beautiful and gentle energy, except when it comes to squirrels. They're his nemesis! He was rescued in Washington State and now lives a very comfortable life in Canada. He *loves* nothing better than rolling in the snow and sticking his head in it!

Gracie is five years old and was rescued from a Native American reservation. She was rescued with two puppies and so much matted hair that she had to be completely shaved. She also had two broken back legs and had obviously been abused because she was terrified of everything and everybody. A lot of *love and care* ensued and she became a *loving* member of a family with two elderly cats and another rescue dog.

She is like a little teddy bear with fur so soft it feels like cashmere. She did not look like this when we first got her. She still has many moments of quiet contemplation, but doesn't have a bad bone in her body, even after how she was treated. *She is loving, gentle* and looks like an Ewok with her overbite…a face only a mother could love, but a dear, sweet and gentle companion who also works as a volunteer dog with **PALS**, where she visits the elderly and infirm. As soon as her PALS bandanna goes on, she knows she's going to work! ~**KIMBERLY** ♥

She is loving, gentle and **looks like an ewok** with her overbite…a face only **a mother could love.**

GRACIE

HOW SWEET IT IS!

NORMAN

While I was working on my daily cooking show, they brought **Norman** (Elvis, at the time) into the news station to try to get him adopted.

He was scared, had two front paws like a basset hound and the rest was a mix of basset, beagle, hound and shepherd. It was *love* at first sight! It had been a year since our *beloved* Chester, a Greyhound, had died, so the timing was perfect. We looked at each other and bonded instantly. Not so much when we brought him home.

We found out he had been abandoned in Sebring, Florida, and was terrified of men and thunderstorms. While Norman and I became attached at the hip in less than a week, it took him a few months to realize that men in this new home were full of love and *cuddles*.

He has been my soft and loving companion for over eight years now and not a day goes by that I don't feel surrounded by that canine *affection* and undying protection. ~**JUDI** ♥

so cute!

A FAMILY AFFAIR

NICHOLAS, SPEEDY THE ROOSTER & CLEO THE ONE-EYED KITTY

KRISTOPHER & ADMIRAL BUTTER

NICHOLAS, GOOSE & NOLLIE & FRIENDS

NOLLIE, BANSKY, ADMIRAL BUTTER, SIR WINSTON, GOOSE & THEODORE

My son Nicholas *adopted* **Nollie** when she was a puppy and he named her after his friend Nolan who had passed away. This is how he celebrated his friend's life. As his mother, I thought that was remarkable.

Bansky, the little teacup piggy, belonged to my son Kristopher. He got Bansky—named after the graffiti artist who wears a black hoodie—so his boxer, Admiral Butter (who is the son of Nollie) would have a *playmate*! I think he thought it would be easier than getting another puppy. Teacup pigs are supposed to max out at 35 pounds. At 130 pounds, the boys stopped picking up Bansky and stepping on the scale! He did not like to be weighed. He is three years old now and I hope he has stopped growing. He uses a doggy door to go in and outside of the house. He is the love of my life! I found out pigs live about 20 years. He resides with me now and I couldn't be happier!

Sir Winston is a Cardigan Corgi and was named after an English gent! Since the Queen had corgis I had always wanted one! He is 11 years old and is my constant companion. Always underfoot! He's

NICHOLAS WITH NOLLIE

GOOSE

GIAMPIERO & SIR WINSTON

ADMIRAL BUTTER & BANSKY

ELIZABETH & BANSKY

the best dog I have ever had, so *loyal* and *obedient!* Nollie is our son's dog and is staying with us as her "husband" Goose, his other dog, had surgery on both hind legs! Goose is a special dog. But he must remain calm and not move much so we are caring for Nollie for two months.

Goose was saved by my son Nicholas at a pet store in Colorado where the owner gave six dogs just one bowl of food to share! Of course, some dogs received nothing. Nicholas was horrified and bought the puppy right then. Goose is more human than dog. Note the way he sits! He just endured hind-leg surgery, as both his ACLs were torn. He is the *sweetest dog ever*. We hope to have him around for a very long time!

Theodore came to us via the pound. He was a Christmas gift to me from my college-age son! Best cat ever! We have nicknamed him *Theodorable!* He loves to be able to touch us when we watch TV. We think he is about 12.

Our pets are family and, as such, they are loved and pampered. ~**ELIZABETH** ♥

BLACKIE

BLACKIE & PIPER

My two fur babies, **Blackie** and **Piper**, came to us on January 16, 2013. It was a snowy day and they showed up around 9 in the morning. My husband, Michael, was out in the yard and the little black one ran across his path, followed by the brown one, and they headed straight to our front door. Michael came to get me and said, "Do you want to see the *cutest* thing you will ever see?" I was busy at the time and said, "What is it? A deer? A turkey?" It was *love at first sight* but Michael said not to feed them or they wouldn't go home. So I just petted them and left—thinking they would be off on another adventure. But they stayed until 5. (I did sneak some chicken out to them at lunchtime!) By then it was getting cold so we brought them into the mudroom and put a sheet of foam insulation across the doorway into the house and I went to town to get a little box and some food. They tried desperately to get to us, scratching the foam and trying to jump over, but they were still pretty small (later, the vet said they were about 4 months and four pounds). We put posters up at the local store and PAWS and searched a radius of neighbors but no one came forward

in a 2-week period. My concern was that a little child or an elderly person would miss them but the vet said it was fairly common for people to see a farmhouse and drop them off. I was in *love* after two days and have always seen them as a gift from God.

Blackie and Piper came at a very difficult time in my life. We had been going through moving my elderly parents into a new home and renovating it as well, and we had just moved into our home, which we were also still renovating. Blackie and Piper brought such *levity* and *life* into a very frustrating and overwhelming time.

Blackie can't meow. The vet said her throat had been damaged (birth or human hands?) but she chirps and makes the *loveliest* sounds instead of meowing, which her brother Piper more than makes up for. He is our "chatter."
~RHONDA ♥

PIPER

LONGTIME COMPANIONS

MARLEY & SHAWN

MARLEY

Marley, an Australian shepherd/border collie mix, was adopted from the SPCA when he was 13 weeks old. His new owner, Shawn, was 18 years old at the time and a college freshman.

It was love at first sight and the two shared a beautiful bond that spanned 15 years and included a separation and *joyful* reunion when Shawn returned home from serving his country in Afghanistan.

On March 27, 2017, Marley went to the Rainbow Bridge after bringing so much *happiness* to not only Shawn but his entire family as well. He will be forever remembered and loved—our *heart* dog for life. ~**KIMBERLEY** ♥ *(Shawn's mom)*

It was love at first sight and the two shared a **beautiful bond.**

THE CHINA SYNDROME

OLIVE

My dog is named **Olive**. Her given name, when she was rescued from China, was Faith, so now she is Olive Faith.

Olive was rescued by a wonderful man I met through Facebook. I am a huge *dog lover* and firmly believe in rescue and adoption (*#adoptdontshop*) and saw this amazing guy, Marc Ching, who was in China on a mission to check out the dog meat trade over there. He ran a small rescue at the time in Sherman Oaks, California, *rescuing* severe abuse cases. But he wanted to do more. So he went to China.

One day when he was outside a terrible dog slaughterhouse where they torture dogs alive and then slaughter them, he heard a cry. In a dirty culvert of mud and sewage was a small plastic bag. He tore it open and discovered four small poodles, each about 1½ pounds at most. Olive was one of them. Unfortunately one had already passed. He grabbed the other three (after burying the deceased

one) and rushed them to the nearest vet emergency a few hours away. One of Olive's siblings passed away during the car ride, and the two remaining were hospitalized for weeks. The third poodle passed away after a few weeks. They were all very sick with respiratory illness, and Olive was also extremely sick. She hung on by a thread and finally, after eight weeks, she *recovered*. She was sent to the USA in early December and landed in Los Angeles. I drove down from Los Gatos, which is about a 6-hour drive, and picked her up.

She is truly a miracle dog, surviving odds stacked against her from the minute she was born.

Olive is now 2 years old (I got her at 3 months). She is *thriving* and very happy and lives with three rescued sisters, a rat terrier, and two mutts. ~**JUDY** ♥

About Marc Ching Marc Ching's heroic efforts have not gone unnoticed by more than one million people and fans who follow his inspiring yet dangerous plight on social media. Now a headline-grabbing animal activist, Mark has been the subject of stories and profiles on many prestigious media outlets including CNN, CBS News, ABC News, Entrepreneur, The New York Daily News, The Huffington Post, Buzzfeed, The Dodo and more.

Please take a look at Marc's website, Animal Hope & Wellness (*animalhopeandwellness.org*) and his Facebook page: *facebook.com / animalhopeandwellness*.

HEALING SPIRIT

ALTHEA

Althea appeared at our front door *meowing* in August last year, just skin and bones and bedraggled as anything. You could feel her spinal column and ribs. She had horrible puncture wounds on her neck too. My daughter Ellie, who is a vet tech, and her dad, who is a veterinarian, both think she was possibly picked up by a large bird of prey and maybe dropped or somehow must have gotten away.

Anyway I gave her a few treats, which she eagerly took and ate right away. Then we gave her dry food and she ate that, too. So we brought her in and separated her from our other cat, Willow, by putting her in the bathroom for the night. We had to keep the kitties apart with baby gates for about two weeks before we felt Althea could safely be in the room with Willow. She must have mostly slept for at least a month after we got her. She was so traumatized and worn out from her ordeal.

It took a long time for her neck wounds to heal, even with meds. So I fashioned a soft little collar out of a sock to wear around her neck. Ellie said that judging from her looks she had been on a long journey. And she told me, "Mom, she found *you*!" Even to this day, Althea runs away from the door when we open it. She does not want to go outside! She was 3-5 pounds when we got her and she is now a whopping 13 pounds. In fact she is on a little bit of a diet at the moment!

Althea means "healing" and it is the name of the marshmallow plant, which has healing properties. She *adopted* us during a difficult time in my life, and her sweet spirit, her *snuggles*, and her pretty funny little face make me laugh all the time, which is so therapeutic. Indeed, she is a very healing little creature to be around. We *love* her (and Willow too!) ~**CINDY** ♥

Her **snuggles** and her pretty funny little face make me **laugh all the time.**

THE GOOD LIFE

COOPER

We adopted our **Cooper** from Faxon Animal Shelter in Fall River, Massachusetts, in 2004 when he was about 4 years old.

He is a shorthair Manx with a little stump of a tail. He is now around 18 years old suffers with chronic kidney failure.

He is such a *sweet boy* who *enjoys* several brushings a day.

We are fortunate to have him in our lives. ~**DEBBIE** ♥

NEVER SAY NEVER!

DAISY & MAGGIE

We adopted **Daisy** because a few years earlier we had lost our beloved West Highland white terrier to age.

I said I would never get that attached to another pet, but when I saw Daisy I had to have her and couldn't wait for her to be old enough to bring home. She is now 13 years old and almost blind and deaf but she is greatly *loved*.

Maggie was rejected by her mother. She had a skin condition, was fed with an eyedropper and carried around most of the time. We couldn't resist her! She is *very loving* and a bit spoiled. She is now 7 years old and very loved even though she continues to have serious skin problems and chronic ear infections. She costs us a fortune in vet bills and prescriptions but she is totally worth it. ~**BARBARA** ♥

DAISY & MAGGIE

A GOOD MAN & A GOOD FAMILY

SCOOBY

We had wanted a dog for quite some time but were waiting until we owned our own home. About eight months after we moved in we decided it was time so, as we knew we'd absolutely be getting a rescue, I started checking out all the shelter sites. It was on the Gulf Coast Humane Society site that I saw **Scooby**, a 3 year-old American Staffordshire terrier mix, and fell in *love*. I couldn't stop thinking about him and staring at his pictures! I would even text them to my husband during the day.

We went to the shelter early on a Saturday morning. My husband told me to keep an open mind, that Scooby may not still be there or may not be the right fit for us, so we didn't specify any dog when we got there. Of course, in my head, I was there for my Scooby boy. After walking up and down one section and not finding him we went to the second section and there was his cage. He slowly walked around the corner and my *heart* completely melted. There was no way we were leaving without him!

He was first rescued by Officer Manny DeCastro, who found him living under an abandoned trailer. He was skin and bones and covered in flies. The officer spent weeks bringing Scooby food from McDonald's until he finally gained enough of his trust to get him in the patrol car. He was then taken to the shelter. He'd been in there for nine months (including a failed adoption) when we *adopted* him and definitely came with some issues. He has a deeply ingrained fear and dislike of other dogs so walking him is a challenge but he's so worth it! He has enriched our lives in so many ways and we absolutely *love* him to pieces!

I look at his scarred up paws and often wonder what he went through in the years before he was rescued, but it's probably better that we don't know.

He is *safe* and *loved* now. ~**VICTORIA** ♥

I couldn't stop **thinking about him** and staring at his pictures!

IN PRAISE OF OLDER DOGS

MOOSE & WALLY

Meet my two rescues **Moose**, the blind, one-eyed, Shih Tzu, and **Wally**, the mini poodle. I will start my story with Moose because this little guy was the one who changed my life forever.

MOOSE

My husband and I stumbled upon Moose at an adoption event one afternoon at an outdoor shopping center in a part of town that we rarely visit. It was by chance that we were even there, all because of a pair of shoes my husband needed for a trip and this was the only location that had his size! My husband *loves* dogs and always had one growing up. I, on the other hand, was the complete opposite and was terrified of dogs no matter how *adorable* and friendly people say they are. My husband spotted a little white-and-tan Shih Tzu and wanted me to go see him. I rolled my eyes and reluctantly agreed. The funny thing is, as we were

MOOSE

walking towards the area, I had spotted the same dog that my husband wanted to show me! This moment was the first time we both met Moose and the first time in my life that I had any interest in dogs. There was something about Moose that drew me in. Although I was cautious and a little bit scared to put my hand close to his face, a part of me was very curious about this little dog. Moose's foster was there and we learned that she had been fostering him for four months.

Most people would turn away after they learn that Moose is missing one eye and the eye he does have is completely blind. His blindness did not concern us at all; instead, it did the exact opposite for me. I thought to myself that if he had tried to bite me, I would be able to run from him and he wouldn't know where I went! Thinking back, I realize how silly I was to think that! A few days after meeting Moose, I told my husband that I couldn't stop thinking about the little dog. I'm sure my husband was shocked but he said "me too." We immediately called the *rescue* to get in contact with Moose's foster and asked if he was still available.

With our nuptials being just two weeks away, we told ourselves that if Moose were still available after we got back from our destination wedding we would *adopt* him. Sure enough, he was meant to be our first dog and we adopted him on December 8, 2012.

Moose proved to be the best first dog I could ever ask for. His calm and *gentle*, loving energy helped me get over my fear of dogs and inspired me to rescue more dogs and my sister to adopt her first dog. I started reading more about animal rescues, shelter animals and what happens to animals that don't get adopted. This opened up my *heart*. Because of Moose, I had a soft spot for senior and special needs dogs.

My precious Moose passed away on November 16, 2017. When he was first diagnosed with congestive heart failure, he was given two years to live, but he gave us three.

We all know that the time we have with our fur babies will never be enough but when you get the gift of time, even if it's just one year, it is the best gift you'll ever receive. I am so *grateful* to have been his dog mom for five years. Moose did so much for us and we will take what we learned from him to do more and give back. This gift I received from my sweet Moose is the gift that keeps on giving.

WALLY

I may have had Moose for only five years time but the impact he has made on me will last a lifetime.

WALLY

One day, I was browsing Petfinder online and set the filter to only show me senior dogs in my area. This is how I found my little **Wally**. I wrote down his ID number and off I went to my local animal shelter to find this 11-year-old mini Poodle. I walked around the kennels twice and couldn't find him so I asked one of the workers if he had already been *adopted*. The lady said, no, this dog is in isolation due to a dog bite.

My heart sank as she asked me if I wanted to see him. I said, yes, of course! As she led me into the isolation area, I wondered how in the world would anyone know these dogs are back here? This area was not open to the public and there were so many of them! I met Wally and noticed his dog bite. I knew in my *heart* that I could not leave this little guy behind. I know that senior dogs are often overlooked, let alone one in isolation. I signed the adoption papers without even talking to my husband about it because I just knew that I would rather save a life and let my husband be mad at me than leave the shelter that day full of regret and sadness in my heart.

Wally turned out to be an energetic, joyful, spunky 3-year old little boy and not 11 years old as he was listed in the shelter! He is full of life and completes our family of four.

I hope my adoption stories can inspire someone. Senior dogs' affection is timeless and their devotion is ageless. ~ **EMILY** ♥

UNCONDITIONAL DEVOTION

BEAU, HARLEY & GRACIE

BEAU

HARLEY

GRACIE

I lost one of my beloved dogs, Cooper, three years ago. I thought I would be fine with just my one, original dog, 11-year-old Ellie. But after a few weeks of missing Cooper, I decided to go on the local bichon/poodle rescue site. Up popped **Beau**'s photo! He reminded me so much of my Cooper and was only 15 minutes away in a foster situation. I called the woman immediately and drove over to see him. The *rescue* woman had eight dogs and six cats in her small home. All were in one bedroom in cages. She had Beau out when I got there. He was a shy, skittish, emotional mess. All he did was run in circles as fast as he could go. She finally caught him and handed him to me. He was like a frozen statue yet I could see the love and *heart* in this little boy. She went on to tell me he had been dumped in the middle of a highway after he was used up from breeding. He'd lived in a cage his whole life (6 years) and had no human contact. Four other families had come over the last year to adopt him, but they all returned him as he wasn't the "perfect pet" they were looking for. As we continued talking, little Beau was falling asleep in my arms. The foster woman was shocked and said he had never done that with anyone else; he needed me and I needed him. He filled a void from losing Cooper. I brought Beau home the next day, carried him out into my fenced-in backyard with Ellie and I sat down with him in the grass and let him go. He ran for two hours in big circles, nonstop, only counterclockwise and on three legs! Ha! I just sat there and let him do his thing. Slowly, over time, he started to come out of his shell. He has come so far in his here years. He's still skittish and will still run counterclockwise when he gets nervous but he has brought me such *joy*. He is the gentlest, most *loving* boo ever. He just wants to feel safe and loved. And he is.

Then there is **Harley**, a little 5-pound poodle girl with the *spirit* of 10 high school cheerleading teams! I adopted her from a rescue in Ohio. She has a severe heart murmur and is on medicine three times a day but I was so happy to help her and give her a good ending. And, so far, she is doing really well! I've had her over a year now and her prognosis is looking very good!

Last, but not least, is **Gracie**. She came from a high-kill shelter to the Detroit Dog Rescue where I found and adopted her. A backyard breeder had overbred her. She had one ruptured mammary tumor and one the size of a baseball. The DDR saved her, took her for surgery, but post-op she was found to have terminal cancer. They said she probably has less than a year but I took her in to give her the best last year/years of her life. To look at her you would never know she is sick. She has *blossomed* since being home with me and her three siblings. ~**TERI** ♥

GETTING ALONG

MACIE

Macie is my *sweet rescue dog*. My husband was looking around online and somehow ended up on a site with dogs. He showed me a picture of Macie as a tiny puppy and my *heart* melted. She was in a kill shelter in Arkansas and we were in Connecticut. I called very quickly but a worker said "Hold on, I don't think she is here anymore," meaning she had already been killed. However they found out that Macie was still alive but had been sent to a different shelter because she was about to be killed that day.

At the other shelter and foster home she got sick. It was months and months before she was well enough to take the drive to Connecticut. We paid a service to bring her from Arkansas to Connecticut and today she is a 6-year-old *beauty*. She is the light of our lives. I can't imagine living without her. We have other animals: another rescue dog, Daisy, three chickens, three hermit crabs, fish and of course bunny Jasper (pictured here with her). Macie gets along with each of them.

Rescuing her was the best thing we did! ~**DEEZIE** ♥

He showed me a picture of Macie as a tiny puppy and my **heart melted**.

AS FATE WOULD HAVE IT

KIZZY KISMET

I was outside talking with a neighbor who was introducing me to her new dog. While we were visiting, I kept hearing meowing, and after she left I walked across the street to find this *lovely kitty* that slowly allowed me to pet him! Another neighbor walking her dogs brought over a couple of cans of cat food and by that time he was letting me hold him.

He desperately rubbed his *sweet* face on the cans of food letting us know he was starving. I fed him and before I knew it, I picked him up and let him inside my house. He spent a couple of nights with me and then I took him to Cat Depot to discover he had a microchip. He was registered to Tanks, Inc., an organization that rescues cats. I was ordered to take him to their vet.

The next day I called to ask if he was up for adoption, and he was! In the meantime I was looking to fill in the gaps of his story—the Manatee County Animal Services had picked him up as a stray, and Tanks, Inc. had rescued him. **Kizzy** ended up in my neighborhood when the handyman doing work across the street was here. Kizzy fell asleep in his van, and when he opened the door the cat went flying out! I *adopted* him and named Kizzy Kismet for how we met! ~**PANDORA** ♥

The next day I called to ask if he was
up for **adoption,** and **he was!**

LITTLE ANGELS

Keoni loves them and it's **beautiful to see how gentle** and caring they are with him.

OCHO, LOLA & SNOWBELLA

I rescued my three babies, **Ocho**, **Lola** and **Snowbella**, from a breeder who was continuously breeding the animals strictly for the money and without care or regard for their well-being. I just wish I could have taken more of them home.

I am *blessed* to have them. They have been a constant help and wonderful *companions*, giving so much unconditional love to my daughter, Naomi, and my son, Keoni, who has autism. Keoni *loves* them and it's beautiful to see how gentle and caring they are with him. I can also say that they saved my life: Many articles have been written regarding how dogs can detect cancer in people. Ocho and Lola kept sniffing my lower back, which led to a diagnosis of stage 4 melanoma. If not for them, it would have metastasized, and I wouldn't be here today.

Though I rescued them, I can say for certain that they *saved me*. I am forever grateful for the love and comfort they bring my family and me. ~**STEFFIE** ♥

OCHO, LOLA & SNOWBELLA

FINDERS KEEPERS

LACEY JANE, BUGGY BUGGERSON & GRACIE LEE

Lacey Jane crossed the Rainbow Bridge a year ago. She was our 17-year-old rescue, and probably the kitty *love* of our lives, though, of course, we adore them all. Right after we adopted her from the shelter, at one year old, she crawled into a hole beneath our newly installed kitchen cabinets, and was sealed into the corner unit with no exit for three days until our other kitty, Oreo, heard her. My husband, Steve, had to remove a huge new floor-to-ceiling laundry room cabinet to get her out.

A week later, she jumped high up onto the TV unit, over a candle. Fortunately, her long, lustrous belly fur had been shaved for her spay surgery, and she was fine. She was down two

LACEY JANE

GRACIE LEE

lives in only a week! But she never had another accident. A *lap-lover*, and nurse, we miss her so. (PS no more open candles at our house.)

Buggy Buggerson is our 12-year-old who we rescued from the same shelter at 8 weeks old. Her name is really Julie, however she has a real catitude. *Not* a lap kitty, she *loves* us in her own chosen moments. She is the queen of the hairy eyeball. Buggy likes to sleep on our Mongolian lamb throw near **Gracie Lee**, but she will not be touched. She also likes bugs, hence her revised name.

I discovered Gracie Lee online soon after we lost our Lacey Jane. Steve and I were not ready for another kitty so soon, but her precious face just made me fall in *love*. She was living in a feral cat colony in an old abandoned store 50 miles away, in the country. Her rescuer went and captured her, then delivered her to our home, along with two dozen free-range eggs from her own chickens. **Gracie** was in heaven from the moment she arrived in our home. We have decided that she was never feral, that someone must have abandoned her. She is so very loving and *sweet*, and a wonderful lap *lover*! We truly believe Lacey Jane sent Gracie to us. We needed each other! ~**DEBBIE** ♥

BUGGY BUGGERSON

RUNNING NO MORE

AIDAN BLUE

Here is our **Aidan Blue**. We rescued him from a racetrack where he had been raced extensively for three years. When we fostered (then adopted) him, he had no hair on his undercarriage or hindquarters. He had been kept in a hard, unpadded crate for all of his racing life and was extremely nervous and untrusting when we first got him.

I'm happy to say that he's turned into a beautiful, gentle and *loving boy* who loves to snuggle on the couch (and in bed) and his hair has even begun to grow back. He's *elegant* and fast, but more than that, he's truly a gentle old soul who can also be a big goof!

He loves to *play* with his other rescued greyhound friends, but never wanders too far from us. I also volunteer at Northern California's Greyound Friends for Life, where I walk, socialize, train and spend time giving plenty of love and tenderness to all of the many greyhounds we rescue from racing tracks, abusive homes or the streets. ~**KAREN** ♥

SAVED & LOVED

GRACE AS A KITTEN

GRACE & ROSIE

GRACE & ROSIE

Grace and **Rosie,** my blue-eyed girls, are Ragdoll sisters that we rescued on New Year's Day, 2016. When we got them, they were seven months old (best guesstimate from our vet) and very shy. They were rescued from a hoarder/breeder way up in Northern California, where they (and all the other cats "rescued") were sent to a high-kill dog shelter!

There is this fabulous organization called Purebreds Plus that heard there were Ragdolls at this shelter, so they rallied the troops and went to *rescue* any of the cats that hadn't already been euthanized.

We had just lost our Belle earlier in December. My husband Rick and I have had a cat (or two) just about our entire lives together. There was such a void when Belle died and we didn't want too much time to pass before getting another cat. I liked the idea of getting a sibling pair.

They were so shy when we first got them. I just hate to think of what trauma they endured before they were rescued. We are a *calm* household, and before long they were exploring and getting to know us. They are still shy around strangers but they will warm up to you if you speak quietly. Grace (the darker one) is the more reticent of the two.

She is also more delicate than Rosie, who is very sturdy and a bit less skittish. Ragdolls can weigh more than twenty pounds, but our girls seem to have topped off at the 9- or 10-pound mark. *Ragdolls* have the eponymous characteristic of being super floppy when you pick them up. It's the funniest thing. They are the light of our lives. **~ANDREA** ♥

TEACHING, SHARING, LOVING

OLIVE

This prissy little girl, **Olive**, is now 14 years young! Her life had a rough start, learning how mean this world can be—she was in a puppy mill for eight years, then cast aside to a shelter.

A kind lady and her son saw her, took her home with them, and kept her for two weeks. Being from a puppy mill, Olive had no social skills at all. She was not house-trained and she suffered from anxiety; she just did not know how to relax and be loved. Fortunately, this nice lady took her to a rescue instead of back to the shelter.

Then, on Olive's 8th birthday, my life changed, and a new journey for Olive and me began.

Little did I know what I was in for! This little girl taught me *patience!* I taught this little girl *love* and, hopefully, trust. And we are still teaching each other to this day!

I look forward to sharing many more years with *sweet* Olive. I love my little 4-pound, toothless pup! ~**KATHRYN** ♥

Little did I
know what I was
in for! This little
girl taught me
patience!

WITH OPEN ARMS

SCOUT &
TONY

SCOUT, TONY WILLY, LUCY & CHARLEY

Our rescues, **Willy**, **Lucy**, **Scout**, **Tony** and **Charlie**, are the loves of our lives! Here are their stories. ~**JENNIFER** ♥

SCOUT

My dear friend Stacy, a die-hard *rescuer*, fosterer and board member of Hope Animal Shelter was putting some items in a booth she has at an antiques mall (where all sales proceeds go to the shelter) when a girl walked by with a puppy. She saw that Stacy was affiliated with a shelter and asked for help. She had taken the puppy from her neighbor because they always let their dogs have babies and she was worried the puppy would end up in a bad place. Of course Stacy said "Yes I will help, but you need to give me until tomorrow." They exchanged numbers and went their separate ways. The next day, Stacy called the girl only to find out that the neighbors came and took the puppy and gave her away.

But a few days later the girl called to say she got the puppy back and I went to meet met Stacy and the *cute* puppy, continued on to my house and, within minutes, she was ours. Lucy, our other dog, *loved* her and we did, too. We found out later that **Scout** was going to be a bait dog!

She is truly my *baby*; the human baby we never had. She is small, a cuddler and lets me smooch and dote on her all day. She's my *bestie!*

TONY

We live on a golf course and there are lots of critters that roam around; mostly wildlife, but a few cats as well. I kept seeing this little orange tabby hanging around in our area. He would get close, but not too close.

I decided to start putting out food and water for him to make sure he had a full belly. It was the beginning of December and starting to get cold at night so I made a little house for him, not only to keep him *warm*, but also to give him safety to run to if he were in danger. A few weeks went by and little by little I gained his trust...and I started to become attached!

We were putting up our Christmas tree and had the drapes open to our glass patio doors when we were met with a little orange tabby with his face pressed against the glass watching us. I gave my husband "the look" and he said. "Go ahead, let him in."

He curled up on the sofa and slept and purred. He was a *happy* boy. And that's how **Tony** became part of our family. He is a terror but we *adore* him!

WILLY

Willy came to us from an unwanted litter 18 years ago. He is now blind as a bat and we call him our "vampire kitty" as he seems immortal! He has been sleeping on my head every night since he was independent from his mama. He is a *love bug* but has a bit of an attitude. I think it's because he knows he is so handsome. Willy is our main man. He has brought us so much *joy* and hopefully will be with us for a bit longer but we know the clock is ticking…

We had just lost our soul mate pup Cooper and were completely devastated and inconsolable. We both have never felt such a heart-crushing pain in our lives. We decided to get some fresh air two days after Cooper's passing and ended up at the local mall where they have a Humane Society of Southern Arizona rescue center called Pawsh, and we decided to take a peek and snuggle some *fur babies*. We walked in and there was **Lucy** in a fenced-in area with someone who was interested in adopting her sitting with her. We gushed over her and that was that. The

WILLY

WITH OPEN ARMS

LUCY

continued from page 51
woman who was in with her came up to us and out of nowhere said "I want you to have her!" Our response: "Oh we aren't looking to rescue at the moment, but just wanted to visit."

Then my husband and I looked at each other and knew we should go in and sit with her. I went in first and kneeled down to her and she literally grabbed me with her paw then nestled her face in my lap. I welled up with tears and looked up at my husband and he was full of tears as well. I stayed with her for a few minutes, then my husband sat with her and it was an instant bond. He was *already in love*.

We asked the volunteers her story and it was and will always be heartbreaking. Her previous owners had her since she was a pup and decided after seven years that she "got in the way" and no longer wanted her. They dumped her like she was trash. They also left her with hip dysplasia and extreme separation anxiety.

After all of that, we decided we would "think about it" and left. We made it to the car and before we could turn the key to start it my husband and I looked at each other and said we could not leave her behind, and, a half hour later, Lucy was—and will always be—part of our family.

Our hearts were broken over the loss of Cooper and her heart was broken over the loss of the only family she ever knew. And what better way to honor the life of our *sweet* Cooper than saving another. We *love* her so much. She *saved* our souls when they were so completely broken. She was meant to be ours. This I know.

CHARLIE

I heard crying coming from the bushes across the street from our house. I went to investigate and there he was. You could tell he was sick; making all sorts of weird sounds, drooling, sneezing. It was so sad. You could see that he was craving human companionship. He kept rolling around being friendly, *eating treats*, but every time he ate one he would almost choke. I was torn as to what to do in regard to bringing him in because he clearly was sick. But he needed me and I could never leave an animal in distress. I let him in, made a bed and isolated him in the bathroom until morning. I slept in there with him on and off. My heart was sad for him.

I took him to the vet the next day and he was chipped! I was so happy that I would be able to reunite him with his owner and he could get the medical care he needed. He indeed was sick with an upper respiratory infection and a mouth full of abscessed teeth. I can't even imagine the pain he was in. The vet made a call to the owner and I decided to have them give me an estimate for his medical needs so I could share it with his owner. I was prepared to help them out a bit if they needed me to. I waited...and waited...until three days passed with no phone call.

This cat was not going to be in pain under my care, but a $1000 vet bill was not something I could do. I reached out to our animal control facility to see if they could assist me in any way or give me direction (which honestly is not common) since they are "the pound" and a kill shelter. It was my lucky day because I was told to surrender him and they would give him all of the medical attention he needed. I could leave an adoption deposit and if the owner did not come forward he was ours. So that is what I did. And they kept their word.

Charlie is ours, and he is a healthy, *beautiful* boy. The part of all of this that makes me sick is that Charlie had been adopted from that same facility two months prior to someone who lives in our area. They let him get to that condition and didn't let him back in their home. They never claimed him after numerous phone calls. It's sickening. But now he is safe with us, never to be sick or hungry again.

Charlie is ours,
and he is a healthy,
beautiful boy.

A VERY GOOD MOVE

BELLA

My daughter, Bailey, was 7 years old and had been begging us for a cat. At the time, our rescue dog, Buddy, was battling cancer so I didn't think the timing was right. I had also always been somewhat allergic to cats and was terrified of having one that would destroy our furniture, etc. All of that soon changed!

I follow all of the local *rescue* groups on Facebook and thought that if we could find a cat that was declawed (because I didn't want to be the inhumane one to do it), then I could probably get used to having a cat around. One day, this *adorable*, fluffy gray cat showed up on the rescue page and she was declawed! I thought: "That's the one!" I told my daughter that we would go get her the next morning when the shelter opened.

When we arrived at the shelter they took us to see the fluffy gray cat. We were so *excited*, but to our dismay, she was not a good fit for a child. She was extremely terrified of kids and hissed and clawed the entire time we were there. We felt so sorry for her, but knew that she wasn't a good match for us.

The lady at the shelter walked us through the other rooms and tried to find another declawed cat. Unfortunately, there weren't any. As I sat on the floor with my daughter, trying to give her hope of finding one in the future, I felt like I was being watched. I turned around and noticed this adorable little gray tabby cat staring quietly at me through her window. I don't know how we didn't notice her right away! I said: "What about that one? Can we see her?" The lady kindly reminded me that she was not declawed. I sat and thought for a moment, but couldn't resist the *cuteness* that was starting back at me! We took her out of the cage and placed her in my daughter's lap on the floor. The cat sat quietly and looked around the room. She was extremely *gentle* and loving! It took about 2 seconds for us to make our decision: She was going to be ours!

Bella has been with us for over 3 years now and is the best pet ever! She's *funny*, sweet, playful, and *loving*. She often reminds us of a puppy, so she is nicknamed "Puppycat." She has stolen our hearts! I'm no longer allergic and she has never tried to destroy any of our furniture! We found that supplying her with several scratching posts has kept her from even considering scratching our furniture. Bailey calls herself Bella's "Meowma" and I am her "Grandmeowma,"

Bella is my second child and is a best friend to my daughter. I am so glad that Bella found us. I can't imagine our lives or our home without her! After our dog, Buddy, died, she was there to offer the *love* that was missing from our home. She was certainly not a replacement, but a much-needed addition!

Don't be afraid to *adopt a cat!* Allergies can be remedied, and if you supply scratching posts and toys, cats will leave your furniture alone! I'm so glad that I was able to get past my stubbornness and allow this *loving* cat into our home. It was truly one of the best decisions I've ever made! ~**DESTINY** ♥

SECOND CHANCE

JACK

Our beloved **Jack** is a golden-doodle. We rescued him when he was 3 months old from very bad people.

He was near death but we *loved* him back to health. That was 10 years ago, and we just adore him. ~**DEIDRE** ♥

DOING THE RIGHT THING

MOLLIE & BETH

Mollie was a tiny little kitten running around our neighborhood. She had no mommy. She was alone. I would go outside to feed her and she would run up to the top of the tree and hide. It took months and months for me to finally trap her; it was really cold out and I wanted to get her in our garage. Finally one night, I put the wet food all the way to the front of the garage, pushed the button and trapped her. We had six cats at the time so I found her a really good home, but the night before her new owners came to get her, my husband, Mark, and I went out to see her in the garage and she ran over to her blanket and flipped on her side and looked at us as if to say, "You're not going to give me away, are you?" Mark looked at me and said, "Call the people and tell them we are keeping her." And are we glad we did! She is my *baby*. She follows me around like a puppy dog and wants me to hold her every minute. We *love* her so much. We've had her 9 years now.

BETHANY & MOLLIE

It all started with a picture of three adorable kittens on Facebook. I had just lost Marley, one of my rescues, and Mollie was so sad and so lonely she just walked around the house and cried all of the time, so I was thinking about getting another cat when I heard Bethany's story. She had these three kittens and they got *adopted* but no one wanted her because she was the mommy and already a year old. She was at animal services and they were going to put her down if no one took her. Mark looked at me one day and said: "You know you want her! Lets just go *save her* now!" And so we did.

We didn't know how it would work out with Mollie but knew she needed a friend. We brought **Beth** home let her out of the cage and they never even hissed at each other. Mollie was no longer lonely—she had a buddy back! We have had her for 4 years now. She is one of, if not *the*, sweetest, most *loving* cats we have ever owned. She is the happiest little girl. We cannot imagine our life without her and Mollie. ~**SUSIE** ♥

THE GENTLE GIANT

FORREST

My name is Alley and I am from Wheatley, Ontario, Canada.

This *beautiful boy* is **Forrest**. He is a 12-year old English mastiff. He is an illegal immigrant! You see, he used to live with my cousin and his wife (she treated them both terribly). They were going to divorce and he could not keep Forrest. I told my aunt that we would take Forrest, sight unseen, so she drove him across the border from the USA to us.

He is 135 pounds of pure love. He does not have a mean bone in his body and is very popular with the ladies! He really is a *gentle giant!* ~**ALLEY** ♥

A GIFT FROM NATURE

PERCY

My sister and I took a day trip to York, Maine, in September 2010. We often visit the area to meet up with friends who rent a cottage at Nubble Cove.

I had no idea that I would soon welcome a new family member!

It was so hot that day as we sat on the deck enjoying iced drinks and staring at the blue ocean. Suddenly, a *kitten* walked up the stairs and joined the party as if he had been invited. My friend told me that the kitten had been hanging around every day and had in fact been sitting on the deck when they first arrived. They thought he was homeless; no mother cat or other kittens to be found.

A few days later when I was back at home, my friends called. A hurricane was going to hit York and they feared the kitten would not survive the weather. The cottage owner had a strict no-pets policy so they were afraid to take in the kitten for the rest of their stay. While we were on the phone making our rescue plan, there was a knock at their door. A neighboring couple had the kitten wrapped in a towel. They, too, were worried that he would not survive the storm and they knew that my friends had been feeding and playing with him.

My friends left Maine at 11 PM and drove the little kitty to my home an hour away. They left him in my care for the duration of their vacation. In the meantime, I cared for him and *loved* playing and snuggling with him. It was a few weeks before my friends said they were ready to pick him up and when they came by I burst into tears. I couldn't bear giving him up. He had become my *baby*. We agreed he should stay with me and my two other cats.

Percy has lived with me for 8 years and presently enjoys his brother, Oscar, watching birds from his window seat and tearing up couches and chairs in my living room. **~ELAINE** ♥

I couldn't **bear giving him up**. He had become my baby.

GOATS STORY

CHUBB & LITTLE RED

We moved out to a small farm a few years ago. My husband Rob and I are so *thankful* that we are able to give our boys this opportunity to raise and care for animals. It is good for our souls and all four of us have learned so much!

Today we have 13 goats, two donkeys, two sheep, 39 chickens, one horse and a chocolate Lab named Hazel.

Our goats are our pets and our lawn mowers!

Now, with a few moms in milk, I am going to try my hand at making goat cheese and goat's milk soap! ~**ELIZABETH** ♥

PERFECTLY IMPERFECT

MCTAVISH

McTavish was rescued from a shelter in Irvine, California. He was barely a month old when I spotted him in the back of the cage in which he was housed. In that moment, I knew he was mine. I was hoping all would work out and I would get him. He was just a baby and had to stay at the shelter until he was old enough to be adopted.

What a *wonderful* dog he is! He *loves* his walks, but he must walk up against bushes, curbs or walls as he is meandering. **McTavish** has a certain way he wants to go or he just stops looks at you and then you realize he feels comfortable staying close to the sides.

His legs are too long, his face is too small and his hair is sparse. But **McTavish** is perfect! ~**JO ELLEN** ♥

THE PERFECT FIT

ROSIE

This is our **Rosie**, a shih tzu. She is 1 year old, and we found her when she was a puppy.

My kids had begged for a dog for years and I missed having one around. My son is allergic to dogs so it was hard to find one that would be the right fit for our family.

Rosie *loves* to be outside. She could stay out all day when it's warm. She *loves* to lounge on the deck—she thinks she is a cat!

She is the *sweetest* and we love having her in our home. ~ **SARAH** ♥

SWEET SORROWS

JACK & PIERRE

We rescued **Jack** (a little Maltese) from a Craigslist ad. We were Jack's third owners in his 9 weeks of life. He was from a puppy mill in Kansas and sold for profit each time.

We lost him at 14 years old to kidney failure on December 23, 2017.

He had a great life and he was one of the *sweetest* dogs. *Forever loved.*

Pierre, a 1-year-old Coton de Tulear, was sent to rescue our family during tough times. He is a miracle and we *adore* him. ~**DEBBIE** ♥

SMOOTH TRANSITION

MAXIE   CHICA

MAXIE & CHICA

Along with their mom (who was rescued from a warehouse by a kind-hearted woman in my neighborhood) and two more sisters (four kittens, all girls, no two alike), these little bundles of *joy* came my way when a local shelter I'd left my name with (offering to foster when a hurricane was expected) called to ask if I could look after a little family until they were old enough to adopt. The babies were a month old, born in a closet a block away from me and had just started to do their shaky little walk when I met them. After a blissed-out month of watching them learn to run, climb, play and eat real food, I returned them to the shelter, thinking I'd perhaps adopt the mom since kittens sell themselves. But I really wanted two cats so they'd keep each other company while I was at work. At the shelter, I met a couple looking to *adopt* a single cat (they had their eye on the mom, who was just *lovely*) to add to their household as company for their grown cat. Done deal: I was getting two kittens! This picture was taken the night I brought back the sisters I named **Maxie** and **Chica** (can't tell you why for either, but the names fit); Maxie was nodding off and I caught Chica in a yawn.

Having had rescue cats and dogs all my life, I know well the difficulties that come with not knowing an animal's past. While I would and will always, *always* take in an animal in need, it's an amazing thing to witness how these two, who have never seen a day of hardship in their now 6-year-old lives, exhibit such pure contentment. They come when they're called, "sit" for treats and are excellent companions who trust me so completely that I think it has probably made me a better person. So while there are no tales of triumph over adversity, it's very gratifying to know that I have two really *happy* animals on my hands.

It's a daily reminder of how everything flourishes under good care. ~**JANET** ♥

MAKING MAGIC

BEATRIX POTTER, ROUSSEAU, SALVADOR DALI & FROSTY

ROUSSEAU & BEATRIX POTTER

ROUSSEAU

FROSTY

We live in Maryland and I have two human children. My daughter, Sophie, is 14 years old and my son, Oliver, is 12. My children have a strong bond with all our fur babies. My husband, Jon, grew up with many cats... although I don't think he realized what he signed up for with me!

We drove about two hours from Maryland to Pennsylvania to get **Beatrix Potter** (sight unseen) from a wonderful Persian rescue called Persians Plus. Beatrix (we named her—I'm an artist, so each rescue receives and artist's name) was skin and bones and barely weighed 4 pounds. Her fur had been chopped off because it had been terribly matted. She looked like a *hot mess*.

I fell in love immediately! Beatrix Potter slowly gained weight and her fur grew back (although she hates to be brushed). She is beyond sweet and loving. We don't know her exact age (approximately 8-10 years old, we believe) but she plays like a kitten and *loves* her belly to be rubbed! She gets along beautifully with our other kitties and Georgia, our yellow Lab. She has lost all her teeth yet still eats wet and dry food with gusto. Beatrix Potter is a gift!

Our beautiful **Rousseau** is approximately 3 years old. I found him through Petfinder. He had been left outside a veterinarian's office in a carrier and then taken to a local shelter. When I first met him at the shelter, he was sweet but seemed frightened, too. His amber eyes were so soulful, I knew he had to be part of our family! I love the saying, "Who rescued who?" because every time we add to our family, we feel so much love. Rousseau is a *cuddle bug*, he likes to lie close to you and put his paw on your hand. He is a very precious boy.

Salvador Dali—**Dali** as we call her, even though she is named for a male artist—is 4 years old. She was our first rescue from Persians Plus. Dali had been taken from a breeder under terrible circumstances. Before we brought her home three years ago, she was recovering from surgery due to lack of proper veterinarian care. She was very thin and quite petite. She has an adorable *spunkiness* about her. She *loves* to run and then slide! She has a very unique little meow. We tell her that she is a precious princess. She is my

BEATRIX

only Persian that lets me brush and groom her. We are very lucky to have her in our lives!

FROSTY is a 10 year-old flame point Himalayan. I went with my mom to a small local shelter five years ago after a friend said she saw a *beautiful* kitty that had just been surrendered there. He was terrified when we took him out of his tiny cage to visit. My mom couldn't decide what to do, because he was so skittish. We left him, and the next morning my mom called to tell me she was awake the entire night thinking about Frosty and asked if I would go back with her to adopt him that day! My mother doted on Frosty like her own child! Frosty slept next to her every night and they *loved* each other very much.

On January 4, 2017, my mom passed away peacefully in her sleep. It was very sudden, though, so, of course, Frosty became ours. He was a gift my mom left for me. We say Frosty has been rescued twice! But really he rescued us. He is a true copycat. When he first came to live with us, he truly watched the other kitties playing and followed suit. He gets along with everyone! We did not change his name to that of a famous artist, however he is *sweet* and *kind* and has an elegant flair—I think of him as Manet. These kitties are the light of all our lives! I wish we had room for more. Shhh...don't tell my husband! ~**JILLIAN** ♥

 Living with animals makes **life more magical.**

SALVADORE DALI

RENOIR & STELLA

GEORGIA O'KEEFEE

FROSTY

COMFORTING COMPANION

PIPER

I adopted **Piper** from Tulsa Animal Welfare in September of 2015. We aren't sure what breeds she has in her, but our guess is longhair Chihuahua and dachshund.

At first she was extremely timid but she is very *happy* now. She has had some basic training, and learned a few commands, although she still has a mind of her own! She *loves* to ride in the car to take my girls to school, and to snuggle her people with a blanket.

I have dealt with anxiety and depression and Piper is great at *comforting* me when I need it. **~CHRISTIE** ♥

GROWING UP

MILO & PIXIE

Pixie was one of four pups born in a shelter in Van Nuys, California, to a very forlorn mother $3\frac{1}{2}$ years ago. I saw her picture on Facebook and, at five pounds, she was the *cutest*, tiniest little puppy.

Pixie has developed into a *beautiful* 45-pound boxer with one floppy ear whose favorite past time is wrestling other dogs down to the ground! Her current sparring partner is a 5-month-old boxer named **Milo** I found on Craigslist.

His photo was *irresistible*! When I brought him home at 8 weeks old, he was 12 pounds and today, at 5 months, he is a hefty 45 pounds.

Soon Pixie will be no match for him! **~JULIE** ♥

MILO

PIXIE

GOOD HEARTS DO GOOD DEEDS

ROXY & MISSY

Roxy was found on a road in April 2007 by one of my husband's friends after she was almost hit by two cars! She gave up and lay right down in the middle of the street. She had probably been dumped!

Our friend picked her up and brought her to work. We had another employee that took her and then found out he could not keep a dog in his apartment so he came back to work with her. That's when Charley, my husband, called me and asked if I would like a little brown *puppy*. I went to the shop, took one look and scooped her right up! We immediately took her to the vet who guesstimated that her birthday had been around February 15. He thought she was a cross between a Labrador and a German shepherd.

She is the kindest, most *lovable* girl. She is now 11 years old! She brings us so much *joy*!

As for **Missy**, I rescued her from a guy who had a wagon full of puppies at a horse show. I would have taken them all! She was born the same year as Roxy (2007) but in September so she is 7 months younger. Missy is a mini Australian shepherd. She and Roxy are the *best* of *buds*! And we adore them, too, of course! ~**KATHEE** ♥

LIFELONG LOVES

LITTLE MINOUCHE

FIFI & MINOU

MINOU, LITTLE MINOUCHE, BIG LOUIE & MISS SOPHIE

I have rescued many kitties over the years (too many to share all the photos). I have adored each and every one and my heart broke when they passed on. I would have *loved* to have dogs, too, but I travel too much, so cats have always been my rescues of choice.

About 4 years ago, I adopted **Minou** (meaning "boy cat" in French). He was a magnificent Maine coon who was born with a deformed front paw and couldn't get up on furniture. So, I got little stairs for him so he could get on my bed and on the sofa. He was a most *fabulous* cat. He responded more like a dog than a kitty and always knew how to make me understand what he wanted. When I broke my arm, he stayed in bed with me holding my broken arm with his good paw. Then he got cancer, and died. I was heartbroken.

I waited over a year to adopt another kitty, but I knew there was one (and, of course, more) in need of a good home. I got **Little Minouche** (it means "little girl cat" in French). She was a feral kitty and she had been shot with a BB gun. She was pretty wild and scared of everything. After about eight months she started to *trust* me, and a few months later she slept with me and purred. Those were pretty good signs she felt at home.

BIG LOUIE

I wanted to get her a friend but felt I needed to give her a little more "personal" time. When a year and a half had passed, I went to the same shelter to look for a companion. And there he was: this big, *beautiful* black kitty. I named him **Big Louie**.

Louie has a heart murmur, which made him less likely to be adopted, but I didn't care and brought him home with some trepidations because I didn't know how Little Minouche would react.

I kept them apart for the first two weeks; they got to know each other's scents through a closed door. When I did introduce them to each other, Big Louie was the one who was afraid of Little Minouche! Of course, she is quite the *diva* and wanted him to know she was here first. Louie is so mellow! He is at least twice her size but lets her steal all his favorite spots and food. He is a lover, definitively not a fighter.

It has been several months since I brought Big Louie home and he and Little Minouche are getting along just fine, mostly because he always lets her have her way! Little Minouche is getting more and more *affectionate* with me. I assume it's because she wants to make sure she is still number one! Little does she know I *love* her and Big Louie equally. I used to always have three kitties at a time so, maybe, I will get one more next year. I so wish I could save them all.

MISS SOPHIE

As fate would have it, just about the time this book was set to go to the printer, **Miss Sophie** came into my life. Her human mom passed away suddenly and Miss Sophie needed a loving home. A friend told me about her situation and, of course, I was more than willing to rescue her. This darling Ragdoll came to live with Little Minouche, Big Louie and me! We are all so very happy to have her complete our family. **~FIFI** ♥

LIFE'S LESSONS

SASHA & JAK

During college, our daughter, Janna, volunteered at a local animal shelter. She helped out with cleaning, walking and taking care of the animals.

While Janna was volunteering, a litter of six puppies was dropped off. There was a curly tailed, big green-eyed and playful puppy that curled up in Janna's lap and captured her *heart*. We received a call saying that Janna had adopted that *sweet* puppy she named **Sasha**.

A year or so later, Janna completed her dog family by adopting a retired police dog, **Jak**.

He is now living the rest of his life with his little sister, Sasha, and *loving* Janna. ~**SHEILA** ♥

HAPPY ENDING

MAC

"**Mac**" (short for Mackinac because we adopted him from a Northern Michigan shelter) came to us after being trucked thousands of miles from a kill shelter in Texas.

He had such sad eyes when we got him (this is one of his early photos) but has turned into one of the *sweetest* and *gentlest* dogs we have ever had.

He's been a great brother to our black Labrador, Tucker, and to our two rescue cats. I can't imagine life without him! ~**KHRISTI** ♥

LOVE TO THE RESCUE

MAX & ROSIE

MAX

Max was abandoned by his owners who left him alone in their house when they moved away. Luckily, a friend found him. She called me and wanted to know if I would take him. Of course, I didn't hesitate, and precious Max became part of my life about eight years ago. He is very authoritative, full of life and is the king of the house. He stole my heart on the first day and is the biggest cuddle bug! Max *loves* to have his picture taken. He is a total poser and enjoys his baskets of toys. He travels with me everywhere along with my other dog, **Rosie**, and, like Rosie, he *loves* the sun and enjoys the outdoors.

When I adopted Rosie from United Yorkie Rescue six years ago, she had many psychological problems. She came from horrendous conditions at a puppy mill. United Yorkie Rescue received a call that Rosie was no longer needed. She had been bred so many times and couldn't carry another litter.

ROSIE

She was scared, skinny, didn't know what toys were, didn't know the feeling of *love* and didn't trust anyone. It took about three years before Rosie truly trusted me. Today, she is *happy* and full of personality. She loves to eat, have warm bubble baths and lay by a window where the sun streams in. She enjoys her soft blankets and loves to be tucked into her bed at night. Beds are her favorite place to be so she has three of them throughout my home.

I can't express enough what a gift rescue fur babies are. They are so appreciative to finally experience love, and give you their *heart.* When you look into their eyes, that love is like no other. **~JAYNE** ♥

It took about three years before Rosie truly trusted me. Today she is **happy** and **full of personality.**

ACT OF LOVE

PIA BLEU

Sometimes a rescue does not have to be from an organization. It can simply be a rescue from bad pet ownership. A neighbor did not have a grasp on the care and devotion a puppy requires.

This is **Pia Bleu**'s rescue story at 9 weeks old.

Prior to our rescuing her, Pia's six-hour flight turned into 10 hours with a layover and no feedings allowed during her travel time period. Pia arrived home and her new owner was unprepared for the night feedings called by her delicate condition. She was dehydrated, undernourished and in sugar shock.

My daughter Hannah and I were asked by a concerned neighbor if we wouldn't mind caring for the pup while her owner went to work. What would this owner have done without our availability to care for the pup during his time away from home? Our neighbor stated the puppy did not look well and at that point we gave into this *sweet* helpless doggie's needs and care.

We rushed her to the nearest animal hospital. During her examination, she was removed from my hands for resuscitation. The hours of neglect caused her to need a hospital stay and then home care around the clock.

The financial responsibility for her care was mounting with each return hospital visit and treatments. Her owner was hesitant to continue her care and did not want to be bothered with her needs until she was fit to be returned to him. Hannah and I continued to look after Pia's while her owner went on a vacation! And we continued for 17 more days of her recovery, administering medications around the clock to reduce heart issues related to excess fluids due to her neglected condition.

Pia's recovery was stressful and she *trusted* us to keep her safe. Hannah and I couldn't imagine giving her back her to the owner who obviously did not care enough to personally see to her health needs. We had already invested in Pia's care and *love*. Hannah and I offered to reimburse the owner the cost of her purchase if he would allow us to make her ours.

Pia Bleu was surrendered to us, her pedigreed papers were filed (she is an Italian greyhound) and she became ours. Pia's care and happiness now depended on us, forever, and that made us even happier. We are in *love* with her and she loves us. ~**DORE & HANNAH** ♥

THE SELFIE KING

CHUCK NORRIS

Meet **Chuck** ("Chuck Norris", aka Norris)

I was determined to add another kitty to my family. A week after my 26th birthday, I went on a hunt for a longhair white Persian. I started at the local shelter since my family has always believed in *rescuing* animals. They didn't have any kittens! Little did I know, Chuck was patiently waiting at my next stop. I walked into a local pet store to find a pile of kittens! All were sleeping so sweetly, but I was upset—no Persians.

Something made me go back to the pile of kittens...only one opened his eyes and looked directly at me with his big eyes. I immediately picked him up out of the pile and held him close—my *heart* exploded. Five years later, "Norris" is my sidekick and has some serious moves. He *loves* to play fetch and asks to take selfies on a regular basis. ~**MIA** ♥

LITTLE ORPHANS

CARAMEL

MIGLOU

MIGLOU & CARAMEL

Ten years ago, a little kitten showed up at our doorsteps. We, of course, *adopted* him and named him **Miglou**.

Then, last summer, my mom found two 3-month-old *kittens* in her garden. They were very *friendly* but were infested with fleas. We took them to the vet to get them cleaned. We put posters everywhere to see if someone would claim them but to no avail. Luckily, we found one family who adopted one and my handicapped aunt took the other and named him **Caramel**.

Fortunately, my aunt lives with my parents and their home and ours share a common garden, so Caramel now has two homes. My daughters and I *love* when Caramel comes to visit—but Miglou is not always that receptive! ~**SANDRINE** ♥

LOVE AT FIRST SIGHT

The level of **magic** Harry has brought to Seth's life is **immeasurable**.

HARRY POTTER

July 31, 2010, started out like any other day. But on that particular day a friend of my son, Seth, convinced him to go with her to the Muskingum County animal shelter as she was searching for a companion cat for her kitten.

We had a golden Labrador named Willow (from the same shelter) for 11 years. When Seth walked into the *adoption* room there were many animals, all vying for his attention. That's when he saw him, in the corner of the room: sitting quietly was this *handsome* Maine coon kitten. As he stared back at him he couldn't help but notice the striking markings across his face. Almost like a lightening-bolt scar. It seemed only fitting that he was to bring this kitten home on Harry Potter's birthday. So **Harry** he would be named!

The level of *magic* Harry has brought to Seth's life is immeasurable. Seth may have rescued Harry that day, but, the truth is, Harry rescued Seth! They are inseparable. Harry is a traveling kitty; he loves to fly and never leaves Seth's side. They are the *best of friends* and loved by all our family. ~**JULIE** ♥

HOME AT LAST

NORMAN

I commissioned as a Naval Officer in 2015 at the age of 21, and was regularly out at sea for the next two years. The dream of having a pup of my own had to be put on the back burner for the time being.

In July 2017, everything changed as I received orders to my next duty station. Not only would I be staying in my home of San Diego, but I also would not be going out to sea for the foreseeable future. As someone who had just recently finished a seven months deployment, this news could truly not be more ideal.

That same day, I found myself on the San Diego Humane Society website. I found two dogs on their page that I wanted to visit. I finally had some career stability for the next two years so why not go say hi to some *cute* dogs?

A mere hour after my casual web browsing, I found myself actually at the Humane Society, not ready to do anything other than *play* with some puppies. I provided the two names of the dogs I wanted to see and was taken to see the first one: a Chihuahua mix named Job.

As one of the wonderful Humane Society volunteers introduced me to this sweet dog and gave me his background, I was truly beside myself. Job had been severely neglected and abused and had been forfeited not by his owner, but by their neighbor. *Sweet* Job was so timid—I sat on the floor for 10 minutes before he was able to come up and say hello. Several treats and a few belly rubs lat-

NORMAN & FRIEND

er, he slowly was warming up to me. The volunteer asked if I was ready to see the next dog, and I informed her that wasn't necessary. I wanted to take this one home (so much for just looking!). I knew I had to do something about his name—he was absolutely not a "Job!" To my mom's credit, she came up with the idea of naming him **Norman**. To this day, I don't think there is a more perfect name for him! Three hours after my casual web search began, I was walking home with the *sweetest* Chihuahua-greyhound mix named Norman. Ever since that wonderful day nearly a year ago, I have not been able to picture my life without my little Norman!

Norman deserves the best possible life after what he has endured. He fills all my days with so much happiness, and I cannot imagine my life without him. ~**JULIA** ♥

THE HAPPY MANAGERIE

SHARON &
THE DOGS

MIMI

MISSY, MAUI, BUDDY, PAO, MIMI, TIMMY & TABBY

Meet **Missy**: 12 years ago, I found this little girl in a dumpster behind my office. I remember it clearly because I had just finished a broker's open house on my first-ever listing (I was a newly qualified realtor). I heard her crying and couldn't believe my eyes at the sight of this little thing!

I managed to get her to trust me by offering her a piece of cake that I had been saving for my own lunch, and got her in to my car! She was tiny and skinny, her coat was matted and she had a cut on her head, but from the moment I saw her, I *loved* her!

I truly believe we found each other. I had not long arrived in the United States after marrying my husband Steve, and I had lost my mother just previous to that. As I drove from the open house I remember thinking, "I hope my mom can see me…" Then I found Missy. From that moment on, and still today, when she looks at me she *heals my heart* and soothes my soul. I couldn't *love* her more if I tried.

Maui was our next rescue, and was just the opposite situation from how we found Missy. Maui came from a multi-million-dollar home of clients of my husband, who had bought her as a puppy while in Maui, hence the name, but found that when they returned to California, this little puppy needed more attention than they and their staff could give her. She was an anxious little thing—likely having been taken from her mother and spayed too early—and had lots of potty-training accidents in the house. As a result, she was confined to a small kitty container in the kitchen with the chef! They knew we had Missy and asked if we would like to take Maui as they were looking to find her another home. Of course when I saw her and heard the story, Maui joined our household and has been *fantastic* ever since. Maui, unlike Missy, came to us with a little bag full of clothes, a bed and doggy jewelry!

My husband found **Buddy** wandering on the road near our house. He stopped his truck to see if the dog had a tag or anything to identify him, and the dog promptly jumped in the truck! It turned out that he did have ID but when we found the owners we learned that they didn't want him any longer and had just let him go! Poor dog seemed to have had such a hard life; he had clearly been ill-treated and would recoil when you would put your hand out to pat him. We couldn't bring ourselves to give him away so now we were a three-dog household!

Pao was another puppy, bought by clients of mine this time. These clients had bought Pao (like "POW!") with the best of intentions, however, when their marriage failed and they separated, no one could quite take care of Pao with the care he needed, so they asked if we could take him and find him another home. We fully intended to foster him until the rescue that I sponsor could find him a home, and when the day came to take him to his first adoption event, I dropped him off...but when I looked at him in the crate...this dog that had just been so *happy* playing around our house with the other dogs and looked lost and afraid as he watched me walk away. I sat in the car for five minutes then went back in and brought him home! And then we were four!

Every year we are involved in sponsoring and raising money for an animal rescue event called Wag 'n Walk, here in Simi Valley, where we live. Our dogs are all well known to the local community, and the real estate community, for their involvement in our fundraising activities and marketing. They have also become welcome guests in many of Carmel's best establishments, where we go regularly to give everyone a little break!

But that's not all! We do have quite the little menagerie! We got our lovely **Mimi** as a kitten in 2005 from a cat rescue in the valley. She was this fragile little runt of the litter and she was curled up in the corner as all the other kittens played around. We picked her up and just felt she needed us. She has *thrived* ever since and now has claimed my office as her domain and retreat from pesky dogs when they decide to annoy her!

Timmy the turtle is an orphan who wandered up our driveway one day four years ago and never left! After putting up flyers trying to find an owner, no one came forward, so Timmy was given a home in our lily pond, where she resides today.

Tabby is at feral cat who adopted us when she was a kitten and sleeps on our porch. We feed her and make sure she's healthy. She's very vocal and will be sitting at the door at 6 every morning and night without fail, meowing for her food. We were able to catch and release her so she could be spayed, otherwise we get the occasional *snuggle* and are allowed to pet her only when she feels like it, but she has to come to us first, that's her rule!

I think word must have gotten around that The Staples Household was the place to be!
~SHARON ♥

TIMMY

TABBY

AN UNLIKEY PAIR

KOTA

BOODGIE

KOTA & BOODGIE

It began one boring Sunday when my sister, Mia, my roommate and I decided to go to the Greensboro, North Carolina, Animal Shelter to smile at puppies. I remember saying, "We're definitely coming home with a dog," although that wasn't the plan. But three girls at an animal shelter with no supervision are going to find a dog—that's how it goes! We were looking at the different types of dogs and there he was: **Dakota**, a Tibetan mastiff. I absolutely fell in love. I had always dreamed of having a huge, furry pup but had never pursued it. We took him home. He seemed to have had a traumatic background, but he soon became comfortable with us.

Eventually, he came to live with me and my boyfriend, Mark. Now, over five years later, adopting him is without a doubt the best decision I have ever made. He is always looking out for me, and always right by my side, literally and figuratively. Kota is such a sweet and *kindhearted* pup; I know he was meant for me and me for him.

When I went to pick up Dakota at the animal shelter after he was treated for a cough, Mark went to look around while I was checking out Kota to come home. He came back and said, "I found a dog." I was confused but went to look at this dog he found so fascinating, and I didn't really know what to expect. It was a tiny wiener-looking dog, and I laughed. I remember telling him we weren't taking home a little Paris Hilton dog; they are ornery and whiny and obnoxious. Turns out I was right, but a week later we ended up with **Boodgie** & Kota. While Boodgie is *sassy* and ridiculous, he is so cute and fun to snuggle, you just can't help but love him to pieces. Boodgie and Dakota, despite their obvious differences, have become best buddies. ~**JENNY** ♥

WHAT'S IN A NAME?

DELANEY & OAKLEY

We adopted **Delaney** when I was still in college. She had been at a kill shelter and was rescued by a local family. But they already had a few dogs and cats, so they couldn't actually keep her. She was so *adorable*, though, that they couldn't leave her there. She is a Shepherd mix and was named after a Jack's Mannequin's song, "Miss Delaney." ~**CHRISTINE** ♥

Adopting **Oakley** was actually a funny story. We received an email with his picture and story from a close friend.

He was at a rescue in Kansas City and we were living in Chicago where Christine was going to pharmacy school. Not being from the Midwest, she didn't realize that Kansas City and Chicago weren't right near each other. So she thought "No big deal, we'll just go pick him up this afternoon."

Needless to say, we fell in *love* with him and were more than willing to find a way to get him. He is a German shepherd mix. We named him for the street we lived on at the time. ~**KEVIN** ♥

GROWING FAMILY

OSCAR & MACEY

Oscar was adopted from the St. Paul Humane Society by my daughter, Rachel, and her family just over a year ago. The transition was seamless for Oscar and the entire family—*bonding* was immediate.

Oscar loves to play Monopoly with his "brothers," Henry and Owen (they have a system for Oscar to note his preferences while playing the game).

My son, Adam, and his wife, Laura, adopted **Macey** two years ago. She was one of six puppies born August 27, 2016, in a shelter in Alabama. Macey's mom is a boxer; through genetic testing it was discovered her dad might be a foxhound.

The Across America Boxer Rescue group *rescued* Macey from the Alabama shelter. She then moved to a foster home in Indiana until Adam and Laura adopted her on January 31, 2017. ~**TERESA** ♥

OWEN & MACEY

OSCAR

Oscar **loves** to play Monopoly with his "brothers," Henry and Owen.

LOVED TO THE VERY END

PATTY CAKE

We rescued our sweet senior **Patty Cake** almost three years ago, not from abuse but from someone who no longer wanted her because of her age and her health issue. We took her in, had her treated for heartworms, and, after loving her for one year, we discovered she had Cushing's disease.

We once again continued with her daily medications, and kept on *loving* her with all of our heart. In turn, we were her world and she *loved* us back in ways that let me know that she was the happiest she had ever been.

Unfortunately, we lost her due to complications from her illness, just shy of having her with us for three full years.

She was the *sweetest* and happiest baby we have ever had, and though I miss her so, it makes my heart *happy* to know we enabled her to live out her senior years being loved and cared for. ~**CATHY** ♥

LOVE'S REWARD

RUMMY

How **Rummy** came into my life: I feed all the strays in my neighborhood. At times I would have eight or more on my porch; mommas and their babies.

The year I lost my dear husband unexpectedly in May, a new litter of kittens appeared. I fed them as usual.

In November of that same year, when I went out to feed them, one was lying down, not moving much at all. I picked her up. She was like a rag doll. I took her to the vet the very next day. She had an abscess on her back that broke open, and the opened hole had to be stapled shut. I nursed her back to health and she joined my two other kitties, Whiskey and Sanka.

I truly believe my hubby, Bill, sent her to me to take care of and to heal. My heart was so broken from losing him. He sent her to me to nurture and *love*, and receive her *love* in return. She has brought much *joy* to me and I am so thankful to have her. ~**CINDY** ♥

KEEPING THEM SAFE & LOVED

HANDSOME, ROOF TOP, MR. DARCY, OLIVER & GIGI

ARRIETTY AND HANDSOME

Handsome was not only beautiful and sweet but truly handsome of spirit as well. He went through quite a metamorphosis from the day we found him out in the cold and rain.

In the photo I'm sharing, he was 17 years old and not feeling his best, however he allowed my little granddaughter Arrietty (age 2) to give him as much *love* as she wanted and he always reciprocated. It was only a couple of months after this photo was taken that we had the heartbreak of saying goodbye for now until we meet again.

RT, short for **Roof Top**, passed away but her story is worth being told. She started out her life in the home of abusive and destructive people. She ran away and lived on the top of a roof. I heard her pitiful meows and saw her up there and did everything I could to get her down, including calling the fire department and even having my husband beg the homeowners to let us use a ladder to try and get her down.

She subsisted on moths and other insects and drank the condensation off the rooftop air conditioner. Day after day, week after week, I saw her getting thinner and thinner, knowing that it was just a matter of days before she would fall to her death. The grief it caused me seeing her every day (the roof was directly behind our home) was pure anguish. I would open cans, shake dry food; I would call to her, beg, plead, pray and tell her it was okay to trust me. Eventually is was

turning cold and we were expecting snow. And then I saw her do what I didn't think she would be capable of doing: She found a way across a limb, took a huge leap onto my fence and ran toward me! I picked up her skin-and-bone body and brought her immediately into our home. She was an emaciated, very ill kitty. We were able to *love* her and nurse her back to health. She enjoyed a very long, beautiful life with us to almost 20 years old when she passed away. She was such a loving and amazing kitty, our RT!

There is no substitute for the power of *love*, nurturing and consistent good feeling for transforming an animal that has been mistrustful, abandoned and left to fend for itself into a *sweet*, loving pet. We still miss Handsome and RT so terribly. But we still have our beautiful Mr. Darcy, the Maine coon, Oliver and Gigi, who were all rescues.

It's as if they always know where to go to receive *love* and find a home. My daughter and son-in-law saved Gigi from some teenagers who were about to kick and punch her to death. She was only a baby and she never grew past the size of about a 6-month old kitten, even though she is over 5 years old now. She has little bits of scarring around her mouth but she is the *dearest* little girl! Oliver was born feral. Our daughter has his brother, Jack. Ollie is the clown of the family and provides lots of fun and entertainment! We *adore* our rescues, past and present. ~**APHRODITE DEE** ♥

A BOY'S PAL

TUCKER

We adopted **Tucker** two years ago. We saw him on a rescue site on the Internet, fell in *love* with his beautiful eyes and drove three-hours to another state to get him.

I have four boys and two foster daughters. Tucker is very *protective* of all of them. He's very loved and he loves us!
~**ANNETTE** ♥

A HEARTBEAT AT MY FEET

The real rescue story is that she **rescued me**, of course.

HONEY

This is my *sweet* girl, Honey. She is a Chihuahua/terrier mix. We found her on Petfinder. A local rescue had gotten her mom while pregnant from a high-kill shelter. The puppies were born in foster care. The real rescue story is that she rescued me, of course.

My kids and I *adopted* her after my twenty year marriage to their father abruptly ended. She slept in my bed from the first night we had her. I woke up on the first morning with her draped across my neck like a little scarf.

How can you be sad and lonely when you have a puppy scarf? She is now the *baby* of the family. We are so very *thankful* for her. **~JULIE** ♥

HOPPING TO HAPPINESS

JACK

I've had dogs my whole life. After my dear standard poodle passed, I waited a year, but I was feeling the need for a new companion.

I visited a local no-kill shelter and saw a dog by himself, lying in a pen. Several toys covered his bed but he looked like the saddest creature I had ever seen. I called him over. He hopped over, and I noticed he was missing one his front legs. I asked if I could take him for a walk, and immediately I felt a *bond*. I had never had a rescue dog, let alone a 2-year old rescue dog that was also missing a leg! I found out from the staff that he had been adopted once, but the family had returned him. I called my husband, Ted; we brought **Jack** home and resolved to make him feel at ease.

The next day, I noticed my Ted's slippers by the door. I called him at work, and he said he had not left them there. The following day, I found only one slipper by the door. On the third day: no slipper. Jack had learned he no longer needed to work his way into the family. We were wrapped around his paw. Jack now runs our house and herds the four cats that our children have each brought into our home. ~**KAREN** ♥

SPREADING THE LOVE

THEODORE

LUCY

THEODORE, LUCY, GEORGE, VIOLET, CHARLIE & SAILOR

Theodore is 3 years old. My youngest son's friend had a cat that had kittens (I offered to pay to have their cat spayed afterwards). Theodore was the runt of the litter and the last to be picked. My son, Grayson, said he wanted a "bedroom cat," meaning a cat that would be with him 24/7, sleeping and playing in his room. Well, Theodore had other ideas. He is our only cat who goes outdoors. He should have been named "Houdini" because he escapes through your legs when you're answering the door or popping screens out of windows—not exactly the "bedroom cat" my son had had in mind! And, he has the audacity to come to the second-floor bedroom windows in the middle of the night, crying to be let in! But he's a *big baby*: He kneads the crook of my arm for hours at a time.

Lucy is 14 years old. My daughter picked her out from the *adoption.org* website for her 14th birthday. She's a rare female orange-and-white-striped kitty (most are males). She is the *sweetest* cat… and the absolute laziest. When she sleeps, she snores so loudly you can hear her from three rooms away. When it's cold, she will stand in front of the fireplace and wait for you to light it. She won't move until you do. She'll just stare at you for as long as it takes.

George is 10 years old. He has the most gorgeous blue eyes and is a *true gentleman*. He will wait for all of the other cats to eat before he does. Sometimes we call him "Pepé Le Pew" (the love-struck skunk from the old Looney Tunes cartoons) because he gets this romantic look in his eyes, tilts his head to the side, rubs up against you and lays on you for hours while staring into your eyes. If we don't have time, we warn one another: "Look out for George! He's Pepé Le Pew-ing!"

Violet is also 10. We had Violet for two years before re-homing her. She was very, very shy and spent her days hiding under the bed. We felt there was too much activity in our home with kids and other animals, and found a perfect home for her with a young woman nearby, Holly. Holly was single and lived alone. She would come home from work every day on her lunch hour and spend time with Violet. She would even take her on cross-country road trips. They were the best of friends and I thank Holly for giving Violet a home where she could feel safe and come out of her shell. Sadly, about two years later, Holly was killed in a car accident. Holly's parents took Violet in and they say Violet has saved them. She brings them so much *joy* because their daughter *loved* her so much.

Charlie is a cocker-Lab-basset mix we adopted when he was 2½ years old. My oldest son was 9 and would talk about the day he would finally be able to get a dog. He said he wanted to name his dog Charlie, so we had to find a dog to fit the name. We weren't quite ready to adopt a dog, but I thought I would see what was out there. I came across a picture of a dog named "Custer" who was being re-homed privately but an adoption organization was helping. I called the adoption people about Custer and was given his current owners' phone number. I called and asked about Custer. The owner said "Who? Oh, the adoption organization renamed him on their website. His name is Charlie." I was speechless. I told Charlie's owner the story and we both agreed, sight unseen, that we would be the ones to give Charlie his forever home. Sadly, Charlie passed away Valentine's Day, 2017.

VIOLET

We adopted **Sailor** when he was about 7. He's now 12. I have never known such a needy doggie! He needs you to *love* on him 24/7. He is never ever without a stuffed animal in his mouth. I call him my huge, four-legged toddler because I clean up his toys all day long. They are everywhere. But we *love* them all! ~**KAREN** ♥

SAILOR & CHARLIE

GEORGE

LOVE & DETERMINATION

PEACHES

This is **Peaches**, rescued from the Carson shelter in Southern California. This was no easy feat, because I live in Illinois. It took a village of *wonderful* people I had never met, and still haven't met, all accomplished through Facebook. It was difficult because shelters do not want to work with people out of state, and many rescues don't, either. But I just kept reaching out to people, and networking and begging and pleading for help.

Peaches had been in two shelters and came in as a stray with part of a chain still attached to her collar. They believed she lived outside, and was used as a backyard-breeding dog because of her very round tummy. Her time was up at Carson shelter, and no interest had been shown for this mature little *girl* with a graying face and cataracts. I knew I had to do something. I called the shelter, but they couldn't do anything because I lived out of state.

But I didn't give up, and numerous people stepped up to help. It took two months, two foster homes and the participation of many. She has been with me for about one and a half years. She joined her four sibling Chihuahuas, two of whom are also rescues, and five cats that were strays. I have a deep *love* for all animals. They have so much to teach us, especially about love.

I wish this world could have so much more compassion for animals; they are our living companions on this earth, put here to help us learn *unconditional love*. ~**LAUREN** ♥

I have a deep
love for all animals.
They have so much to
teach us, **especially
about love.**

PAST & PRESENT

BABIES

SEPHIE

PUNKERS

SEPHIE, BABIES & PUNKERS

Sephie was a rescue kitty from our local SPCA. Grammie and I would go to the SPCA almost every weekend to look at the cats and kittens, and we fell in *love* with her the moment we first saw her fluffy coat and white booties. She was a birthday present to me from Grammie, and we named her after her. Sephie is either Pennsylvania Dutch or German for Josephine. She was our constant companion for over 17 years, following me around the garden, sleeping against my chest each night and waiting for me at the door when my husband was out of town while working on the road. It was a devastating day right before last Christmas when we had to say goodbye to her. A little section of my yard is labeled "Grammie's Garden" and Sephie is right in the center of it.

Babies showed up in the middle of my garden one afternoon, crying. When she walked out from amongst the flowers, I could see that she had a leg injury. Her front paw appeared to be snapped and dangling. My husband came home about the same time and immediately took her to the vet. We were told she might have to have her leg amputated. But she recovered and became our third cat. I always thought she was sent to me to help ease the future pain of losing Sephie.

Punkers came to me through a desperate plea from someone who also does cat *rescue*. She was feral and about 4 months old. This was one of my hardest cases to crack because she was older. It took me about three months, starting out with leather welding gloves, to tame her. Now, she is one of our *sweetest* cats and is kind of the guard dog in the family. If a fight should erupt between any of the cats she always steps in to stop it! ~**LINDA** ♥

THE CHRISTMAS KITTEN

FANNY PIPPIN

It was a chilly day about 17 years ago when I was in the process of moving. I was packing my boxes into the moving truck when this sweet little tiger cat came lurking around. He was so skinny and tiny. He kept me company all afternoon while whimpering and rubbing up against my legs.

I went inside to get the last of the boxes and when I came out, the *sweet* little darling was in the truck, snuggled up in a box of my vintage linens. I took him out of the box and went inside for one last look around. I was thinking how it was getting late and I knew that I had to get going. I didn't want to leave him there all alone, cold and hungry. I had a strong feeling that he was a stray and didn't belong to anyone.

As I was finally ready to leave, he was there next to the truck, whimpering, almost as if he was begging for me to take him along. So I did. It was the best move that I ever made. Me and my tiny tiger cat **Fanny Pippin** were off to new beginnings!

It wasn't very long after that I needed to register a name for my craft business. I made Christmas earrings for the local craft fairs and I would *donate* all the proceeds to the animal shelter. I immediately named my business after my sweet little baby. Now, years later, I have a popular Etsy shop named after Fanny Pippin. We continue to donate supplies to our local animal shelter every Christmas.

He and I are still going strong. To this day, he is the sweetest, most *loving*, gentle little soul! We will be celebrating his 18th birthday this year. I couldn't imagine my life without him! ~**LISA** ♥

MODEL BEHAVIOR

JESSY

Jessy was my parents' dog. He is Canadian, as were my parents. He is a Yorkie born in July, 2004, in Cape Breton, Nova Scotia, and is now 14. He has arthritis in his legs and has mild cataracts but overall he gets along just fine. My parents both passed in 2008 and at that time Jessy was only 4. They *loved* little Jess and I knew I could give him a loving home so I adopted him. My husband did not grow up with dogs so he had no idea what he was in for. After a week, he was hooked and said, "A house is not a home until you own a dog!" And I couldn't agree more.

Jessy has brought us so much *joy* I can't imagine life without him. He is our special boy and we love him so much. My husband calls him "tippy tippy toenails" as he loves to hear him run and tap his paws on the wood floors.

Jessy *loves* Cheerios and likes to jump on them. He has a teddy bear that he helped himself to while visiting my 2-year-old nephew. That was when Jessy was 4 and we couldn't get it away from him because he loved it so much. To this day that's his old faithful. I have purchased many more since then but Jessy only wants her, his *baby*.

Jessy *loves* the camera too, and is always under foot when I have my camera out. He's my perfect little model! ~**JO-ANNE** ♥

so cute!

WITH A LITTLE HELP FROM MY FRIENDS

Bob and his many friends

BOB

I have lots of *rescue* stories since I moved to a small farming town in southern Alberta, Canada, because the community I moved to has the belief that cats are a dime a dozen. Farmers keep them for mousers and rarely fix them, and the little town I live in was overrun with dumped, abandoned and feral cats. It seemed so overwhelming.

I soon discovered all the local rescues were always at capacity, but I started to try *saving* them, one cat at a time. **Bob** was my first.

I fixed up a doghouse for a shelter and put out food and water to help any strays make it through our Canadian winters. Bob was coming around for a few weeks, but he was too fearful for me to get close to. Eventually he started to trust me after I continued to feed him...and then the temperature dipped down to -25 degrees Fahrenheit. I found him, very cold and crying, at my front door, so I was finally able to get him in to the house. The local rescues were once again at capacity so, 11 years later, Bob is still here. He went from a bit of a meany to a true *snuggle puss!*

It's been a difficult few years because I lost my job and still can't find work so, as a starving artist, I was so *blessed* to finally find a back-door connection to a rescue in a nearby city that now takes any cat I rescue. It has enabled me to rescue hundreds. I'm so thankful to have found them! They take care of all the vet costs, spaying and neutering and then they foster until they find the perfect forever home. We have to keep it secretive because technically they are only supposed to help the cats in their city but thank heaven they are true cat lovers and help the ones I find.

So Bob now lives *happily* ever after with the rest of my fur family: my doggies, Daisy, Lulu and Hudson (two of them are rescues). Lulu came all the way from Los Angeles; needless to say, she's not loving the winters. ~**LAURA** ♥

LOVE & LOYALTY

BUDDY

Our **Buddy** is a longhair Jack Russell terrier.

My boys and I went to the shelter actually looking for another pup to rescue when my youngest spotted this guy. He had been returned twice. I asked why. The lady said that the last time he was returned by an older couple that thought he was destructive. The only destruction I've noticed is that he "nests," which isn't really destroying anything but maybe they thought it did. (Okay, well, there *was* that leather boot, but sheesh, my husband shouldn't leave them lying around!)

Buddy was roughly 1 when we got him; he's now 8. He's not really hyper except for a few minutes when the doorbell rings. He's my dog and thinks he needs to protect me, but he *loves* everyone. He sheds, and, yes, he sits like that all the time. We *love* him to pieces. I would save them all if I could. Rescue animals are forever *grateful*; they will be loyal to you for life. ~**DAWN** ♥

WHEN THE HEART KNOWS, IT KNOWS!

MARY MARGARET

Mary Margaret found her way right to my *heart* by accident. I know a little angel put her in my path. After my beautiful old yellow Labrador, Sunny, crossed the Rainbow Bridge, I recall sitting one day in meditation and asking all my angels to please bring another dog for me to *love*. Talk of divine timing: an hour later, a friend emailed a photo of a black-and-white cocker spaniel that needed a home and, as I usually do, I forwarded it to a rescue, which in this case happened to be the Cocker Spaniel Rescue. This was not the dog for me, but when I went into the rescue's website, little Mary Margaret's face popped up. And I was in *love*. It was such a heart connection! Mary Margaret needed to be *adopted* because the animal services couldn't keep her any longer. Thankfully, the rescue agency assumed Mary Margaret's care until I eventually found her.

The poor little thing had a very painful eye that resulted from glaucoma that wasn't treated, and it had to be removed. She had heartworm disease and other parasites, fleas and a matted, dirty coat. It took me a while (about two weeks) to get connected with the rescue and ultimately about six weeks before I could actually get her. I had to fill out an application and wait for their call. I left several messages but we never got to connect. Days later, I just knew I had to try again. I couldn't stop thinking about this little face. When I finally got the rescue on the phone and they said the foster person she was with was going to adopt Mary Margaret, I cried and hung up with a heavy heart. Although I knew that she was safe and she would have a home and someone to *love* her, I could not let go of that little face. So I gave it a few days and I called back.

I knew I had to just speak from my heart and explained how I felt such a connection to this *sweet* little one. The rescue coordinator listened with great care and said she would call me back in a few minutes. And she did: "Congratulations, Lisa. If you would like MM she is yours!" Apparently there were many dogs in need of a good home at the time as there was a fire at one of the rescues' homes and they were looking to place many other *sweet* dogs, so that particular foster parent ended up taking in another dog. I cried with joy as two sweet little souls got a loving family.

Mary Margaret has been with us two years. She has come along way. With the help of my vet, and all the love, trust and care we gave her, she finally felt safe here and a lot of her health and behavior issues have been resolved. She was very protective and guarded when she first got here. We think she is around 12 years old. She now gets along with our three other doggies. I was worried they would be overwhelming to her because they are so big. But she held her own and let them know right from the start that she is the boss. Our Labradors all know that she is in charge. She is a mere 22 pounds compared to their 80. We call her Mary Margaret, but M&M and Winky are her nicknames. She has taught me so much about how *love* conquers all, and to never give up when the chips are down. She is a fearless little one. I love her to pieces. ~**LISA** ♥

 I couldn't stop thinking about **this little face**.

BOSOM BUDDIES

NICKI & FLOWER

Both of my fur babies were abandoned. **Nicki** (the dog) is 6 and **Flower** is 2. They are *best friends!*

Nicki seems to be a herding dog and Flower has the feet tufts of fur like a Maine coon or mountain cat. We really *love* them. ~**NANCY** ♥

RAINING CATS & DOGS

RUE, PIGGY, SAM, ABIGAIL, SOPHIE & MORA

RUE

Rue is my sophisticated little lady! She just turned 1 this past December. *She is my love!* And there is no love like dog love!

Rue was my 2017 Valentine's Day gift from my daughter and husband. She was born in Kansas City, Missouri. My daughter flew her out to me in North Carolina.

I was hesitant to love again, after losing my Sadie Jo of 16 years. The pain was unbearable when she died of old age. So, here is Rue to take up where Sadie left off. Although I will always *love* my Sadie, Rue has filled the void, though she can be quite crazy and stubborn at times. There is truly something wonderful about the unconditional love that keeps on giving.

Piggy joined our family in March, 2015. My daughter knew she wanted to rescue a bully breed, due to the stigma, mistreatment and overpopulation associated with them.

She recalls her visit to the shelter: "When I went to the local rescue, I walked around probably a dozen times before I even noticed him. He was very quiet and sitting at the back of his cage, just watching folks walk by. He was thin and appeared very shy. Once I took him outside to get acquainted, his demeanor instantly changed, and I knew I had to get him out of there. Initially I named him "Woodrow," as he is quite a classy fellow! But I soon changed his name to "Piggy" because he snorts! He shares a home with three cats and *adores* them.

About our kitties: **Sam** was found in the desert in Arizona at 6 weeks, all alone, with a larva embedded in his neck. He was a mess. He was left at a shelter. I went in to make a donation to the shelter and there he was; I adopted him right then and there. He is now 5 and a *beauty*!

We adopted **Abigail**, aka Nurse Abby, at 8 weeks from a PetSmart event in Arizona. She and **Sam** are inseparable. She is called Nurse

PIGGY

SOPHIE

Now she **greets customers,** and sits on the counter every day. She is expressive and **loving**.

Abby because when my husband or I are not feeling well, or one of the pets is acting odd, she hovers and stays on top of us!

I rescued **Sophie** three years ago. She was quite verbal, wide-eyed and a nervous wreck. I took her home and my male cat tormented her until she ripped open a bedroom screen and sat out on the roof. She literally growled like a dog, terrified to be around him. So I decided to take her to my shop. Feeling safe, she was able to relax. She has been living there the past three years. Now she greets customers and sits on the counter every day. She is expressive and *loving*.

Sweet **Mora** is always making friends, even with the cat statues in the shop! She found us in our driveway three years ago. A neighbor had left her behind so she joined our family.

So, there you have it! *We love all our pets*. It truly is a family affair! ~**KIMBERLEY** ♥

MORA

MAKING A HOUSE A HAPPY HOME

ROSIE & LUCY AS KITTENS

ROSIE

MISS ZOE

LUCY

ROSIE, LUCY & MISS ZOE

My kids had always wanted a pet but my ex did not like animals—at all! When the kids and I moved and got our own place, I swear the first thing they asked was, "Can we get a kitten?"

My family always had dogs, cats, chickens and horses, so it certainly wasn't hard to say yes! I really missed having a fuzzy in the house. As it happened, a customer of my little shop on the Cape fostered kitties. I didn't know that at the time but mentioned to her that the kids and I were thinking about adopting a *kitten*. She got a funny look on her face and said, "Wait just a minute!" She ran out to her car and came back with a framed photo of **Lucy** and **Rosie**...holding paws! That picture sealed the deal and the rest, as they say, is history! There was no way to resist those little faces!

Miss Zoe is my new husband, Rich's, kitty (actually left behind by his ex wife). Miss Zoe is sweet, shy and *beautiful* and is probably around 16 years old. I *love* our girls. The house is happier because of them! ~**LIZZIE** ♥

A CHRISTMAS GIFT

SUPER-DUPER COOPER

My name is Maggie and this is my rescue pup, **Super-duper Cooper**!

He is a German shepherd/Siberian mix. We live in Nebraska and rescued **Cooper** from the Dallas dog rescue. We found this *sweetheart* on Petfinder and he was brought to us by a truck driver carrier company in the middle of a snowstorm in the Midwest on Christmas Eve!

How he came to us is a rather sad story, though. We had been fostering dogs in Omaha through a local rescue in town, and at the time we were fostering a blind Siberian husky. We also had two of our own dogs at the time we were fostering; one a Siberian mix, Ava, and the other a very small Chihuahua named Lola. One evening our little Lola died. It was really devastating.

Cooper has helped fill the void Lola left. He was our little Christmas miracle! And we couldn't *love* him any more! ~**MAGGIE** ♥

He was our little **Christmas miracle!**

WHO'S THE BOSS?

SYLVESTER

I co-manage a thrift and gift shop for the good of ASTRO Foundation. We rescue cats and dogs from a small, dated shelter.

Last year we rescued, spayed or neutered, vaccinated, chipped and got adopted 500 animals. And we are a small army!

This cat, **Sylvester**, who is a girl, found us. Scared and hungry, she hid in the bushes for a long time. We fed her, talked to her and she very slowly started to *trust* us.

As you can see, she finally moved in. She does not like anyone other than my husband. And she tolerates me—even allows me to sleep in our bed! ~**BARBARA** ♥

LISTEN TO YOUR HEART

LUCY

This precious girl with the name of **Lucy** was 7 years old when I rescued her at our local cat shelter named Fearless Kitty Rescue. She had been with them a year already after her owner had passed away.

I was there to meet a Maine coon girl but Lucy ultimately made the decision. She wanted and needed to have her own forever home. It was out of my hands at that point and my *heart* led the way. She has been with me now for 6 months and I *love* her to pieces. ~**FAERIELUNA** ♥

HIS FOREVER FAMILY

TILLY

This is **Tilly**, a rescue mutt we got from a local shelter here in Colorado, by way of New Mexico. We think he's a black Lab/collie mix, and he's about a year old.

Tilly was at the shelter by himself with another "lone wolf" hound puppy, sharing a cage that didn't have any names or breeds listed, just a sign that said, "These ones are shy and quiet." He cowered in the corner when we took him out to say hi, and I think the best way to describe it is *love* at first sight, even though he was a little too shaky and shy to feel the same way right away.

He had a puppy cold and tons of eye mucus from crying, and we decided that second to take him home. He was so pathetic and helpless that we had to scoop him up. He hugged his hound friend goodbye and reluctantly, paws dug in the ground, came with us. He wouldn't eat or get too close to us for the first few hours at home, but one second it clicked, and he jumped into our lap (and onto the couch). He realized he was *home*.

He's anxious and nervous, hates car rides more than anything and still hasn't figured out how to bark, but he's the most *handsome* and spoiled member of the family. His puppy cold is long gone, he has a big yard to run around in and chase deer and elk, he *loves* bikes and hikes, he's an official shop dog and he has a family to *love* forever. I'm so glad we rescued him. We can't imagine life without Tilly! ~**LAURA** ♥

PASTORAL REFUGE

TROY

Meet **Troy**, a big black beauty that was rescued from being sold for meat. He isn't trained for riding but he enjoys his days grazing in our pasture with his fellow horse friends.

The horses belong to a couple named Earl and Jeanne; they have five rescue horses on our Sandusk farm pasture, which we provide for rescue horses.

Though he is not mine, **Troy** is very *special* to me. He is always the first one to come to the fence to see me every time I visit him.

My love of animals is strong in my *heart!* ~**CHRISTINE** ♥

HIGH STANDARDS

BUXTON

Bux! *We love him so!* We name all of our cats after players on the Minnesota Twins, and Bux was in homage to the Twins' new phenomenon, Byron Buxton. When we discovered him, we were visiting my in-laws in Valley City, North Dakota, for the weekend. The afternoon newspaper arrived on a Friday with a feature on six cats the local shelter was hoping to place. I took one look at "Ozzy" (as he was called) and was smitten. A 1-year-old orange tabby that was found wandering by the roadside, his scruffy, not-that-appealing photo, lassoed my *heart*. But it was 4PM, and the shelter was closed for the weekend.

Undeterred, I called my sister-in-law and asked if she knew the shelter operators. She did, and promised to contact them on our behalf. On Monday, when we were back to Minneapolis, we were invited to apply for adoption, and to deliver a list of references.

They checked all three references, and I am eternally grateful for my friend Sarah's endorsement: "Are you crazy? Any cat would be lucky to go to them! They love cats!" We drove back to Valley City the next weekend to bring Bux home, and he jauntily stood at the dashboard, looking out as we drove. We have been the lucky recipients of his *love* and *fabulosity* ever since! It is our privilege to love and shelter him. He gives back more than we can give, and sets the standard for unconditional love! ~**KIM** ♥

TAKING CHARGE

ABBY

Fifteen years ago, **Abby** was left in a filthy mobile home (like something on "Hoarders") with her four kittens and one other cat. We kept our motor home at this park and had just returned home from a trip when the manager told me about the six abandoned cats.

The manager and I used a credit card to "jimmy" the door open so I could see the cats. As soon as I saw them, I knew I could find them homes. My husband owned the mobile home park and I asked him to press charges against the man who abandoned the cats. He laughed and said, "Now, let me understand, you want me to press charges against this man and you just broke into his trailer and stole his cats!" I saw his point and dropped my request.

My veterinarian helped me find homes for all the kittens. I kept the two adult cats, Abby and Chloe. Chloe went to the Rainbow Bridge four years ago. I had no idea that Abby is a flame-point Siamese and Chloe was a Manx. I *adore my rescues!* Somehow they always manage to rescue me! ~**BETSY** ♥

PS: I bought Abby the green frog the day I rescued her and she has *loved* it all these years.

CHANCE ENCOUNTER

ALI

My husband and I were eating at a local hamburger dive in our small Texas hometown. The animal shelter was having an adoption day. We were not looking for another dog, but when I saw **Ali**, I just couldn't resist her. She was one of the last in her litter. Her brothers and sisters were much bigger and friendlier and were adopted quickly.

As soon as I picked up Ali, she hugged me tight and made that *sweet* little whimpering sound. She would not let me go. Well, that sealed the deal. We all cried when I signed the papers.

Ali now lives on a farm with a 9-year-old Australian shepard, two ornery cats and about 80 heads of cattle. Ali is the smartest dog, always "smiling" and happy. She *loves* to play with our grandkids.

Ali loves to be carried like a *baby* and my grandson is happy to oblige! I have always had rescued cats and dogs (and a few cows, too!). They are the best. Ali doesn't have the saddest story, but she does have the happiest face! ~**CINDY** ♥

 Ali is the **smartest** dog, always "smiling" and happy.

BUNDLE OF SWEETNESS

DODGER

This is my daughter, Ginny's, rescue dog, a one-eyed Pug named **Dodger**.

He lived on the street for an unknown period of time, but is one of the sweetest dogs on the planet.

He now has the safe and *loving home* he so deserves. ~**MARY** ♥

IN CARING HANDS

CASSIE

Cassie is special. She is my sweet baby girl who has had to deal with so much. My son said God picked her for me because he knew I could give her the *love* and care she would need, and I do.

Cassie had to have a pin placed in her knee before the age of 1. She suffers from a collapsed trachea, making it hard for her to breath sometimes. She has heart disease that will shorten her life. Yet she is a *happy* girl.

I value each day with her and I have since she was 8 weeks old. She is my heart. ~**DONNA** ♥

NEVER SAY NEVER!

CALLIE

MILO

CALLIE, MILO, TOOTIE & ROSIE

Callie and **Milo** are both 8 years old. The record shows that Callie is a mini pinscher/Chihuahua mix and Milo is a Chihuahua/terrier mix

Seven years ago on our way to the grocery store, my husband, Dean, decided to take a detour and see if there was a pet *adoption* in front of PetSmart. I didn't agree since we had just lost Bennie (our beagle mix) at the age of 5 and I was mad at the world!

It was raining, we drove to PetSmart and there was one cage with only two dogs in front of the store. The organization that was taking care of the dogs was called "ARK." Inside the cage were both Callie and Milo. But there was no way I was going to go home with an other dog!

Milo was really active and *loving* his ball; Callie was keeping herself *warm* under a blanket. She was very shy. One hour went by and it was still raining. Dean finally asked me which one we should take home. My answer: "Both or none!"

We used the cash that we had for the groceries and we took home Callie and Milo. The drive back with these two little things was *amazing*, Callie and Milo both on my lap ready to go to their new home. As far as we know, Milo and Callie were both just left at the shelter, reason unknown! We didn't change their names. Moving on…

TOOTIE

ROSIE

Then came **Tootie**! Again on our way to do some shopping and Dean wanted to stop at the pet store. And it was raining, again! There were nine little Tooties in a large pen. I wish we had taken them all home! Tootie, a girl, is the *sweetest* dog ever.

In September, 2017, we found our **Rosie**. We drove to the Labrador rescue of San Diego. There was a litter of five Labrador mix puppies that were found at a construction site. We took her home and she is the clumsiest, *funniest puppy ever*. She doesn't realize how big she is, and she is only 10 months old!

Beware of grocery shopping trips... you just don't know where you might end up and what you will be bringing home! But it's all good, if not for the tummy, then for the soul! ~**RITA** ♥

Which one should we take home? My answer: "**Both** or **none!**"

LOVE & FRIENSHIP COME IN MANY SIZES

KOELLE & SNITCH KITTY

Can I just say that rescues work both ways?

This is **Koelle**. She's the Great Dane that *rescued* my daughter. Overwhelmed with studies and other personal issues, Koelle's presence was not only calming, but also gave my daughter's mind a place to rest. Koelle was thirty pounds at 6 weeks and this had her original owner re-thinking things. However, my daughter had been an equestrian most of her young life, so Koelle's potential size would be an unimportant factor here on our three acres. We brought her home and the *bond* was instantaneous.

Koelle's BFF is **Snitch** kitty. He came to us via Craigslist! My daughter responded to an ad for free cats. What she found was a heart-wrenching basket of kittens covered in fleas with their eyes still shut and no mother to be found. Snitch was having seizures from low blood sugar and malnutrition. My daughter would spend so much money at the vet that the advertised "free" kitten became a not-so-funny joke!

Lots of TLC, and a few days of being bottle-fed bring our story to a *happy ending*. Koelle and Snitch are happy, healthy and *loved*. This is my wish for all animals. ~**MICHELLE** ♥

SNITCH

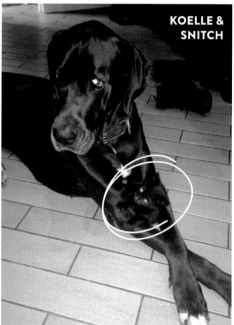

KOELLE & SNITCH

kitty!

We brought her home and **the bond was instantaneous.**

YESHE

I couldn't have been sadder. My Jack Russell had been killed by coyotes, my boyfriend kicked me out of our home and I was driving all my stuff back from Santa Fe, New Mexico, to my home in Florida. I thought, "I need a *doggie* friend!" So as my friend drove the U-Haul, I scanned Petfinder. Somewhere in Texas, I saw these two adorable Wheaton terrier mix brother and sister for adoption near Tampa.

The day after I arrived I drove up to meet them. The sister had just been adopted and there was little Buster. He was so sad! He could barely walk with me. I thought, "Hmmm, the two of us totally depressed...I don't know if this will work." I drove home, realized we both just needed *love* and, a week later, he was mine.

I changed his name to **Yeshe** (which means "wisdom" in Tibetan). Ten years later, Yeshe is still the *love* of my life; happy, funny, super smart.

He and I both found happiness together and I got married to a wonderful man who *loves* him just like I do! ~**NINA** ♥

I drove home, realized we both just **needed love** and, a week later, **he was mine.**

LOOKING GOOD

ASTRO

Astro is 3 years old. We were told he is a Shepard mix (I think because of his coloring). But he is definitely a mix, with some Black Mouth Cur and some pit bull, too. We adopted him when he was a year old.

Once he was in New England, he went to many adoption events, but no one wanted him because he didn't have a lot of fur. But the shelter never gave up on him. When I saw him on the rescue Facebook page, I knew he was the one I wanted to adopt.

He'd been in Florida, where he was emaciated, had the worst case of mange and inflamed paws and was eating twigs to survive. We treated his skin with coconut oil and now it's as soft as butter. He still doesn't have much fur, but we don't care; he is healthy and *happy*, and so are we! ~**MARY ELLEN** ♥

A FITTING NAME

HANDSOME

My name is Stacy and **Handsome** is the cat that adopted us.

I work at a food pantry and thrift shop in a very small town and Handsome lives at our shop. He met us every morning at the back door to be let in and would stay all day. We all fell in *love* with him and *adopted* him.

He is very popular and everyone in town seems to know about him. My customers tell me he is spoiled but I am not sure what they are talking about! ~**STACY** ♥

SWEET AS SUGAR

ROYAL

Since my husband and I were married 27 years ago, we've always had purebred dogs from well-researched breeders. Sadly, most of our lovely dogs died too young. We never understood why, until a bit of research uncovered some of the truths of purebred breeding. When our Newfoundlands died at the ages of 5 and 6 we knew we were done with purebreds. Done with cancer, heart attacks and all the other inherited and horrid things our dogs had bred into them. It took us a year to open our *hearts* to another dog after our Newfie, Teddy, died. We knew a mixed breed would be the best fit for our family. And after seeing a post on social media about puppies in need of *adopting*, we visited a nearby farm.

The pups were filthy, smelly, covered in fleas and clearly had worms. But still, we were so excited about the prospects of a puppy that was not from a professional breeder. Seconds into meeting the pups, a *sweet, playful girl* would not leave us alone. In 10 minutes, two of our four boys who came along decided on her. They named her **Royal**. She is pure sugar. A loving shadow to each of our family members and a wonderful mix of the best traits and spirit from all the dogs we have loved, she has stolen a chunk of our hearts and given us the gift of canine companionship once again. We are certain all the pups we have *loved* over the years have brought us to Royal. And for that and the daily joy and magic she adds to our lives, we are so very grateful. **~TRACY** ♥

TIME AFTER TIME

LUCREZIA, LUISA & LITTLE POLVERINO

My little sister Luisa and I didn't really rescue cats from the shelters but always took them in from the streets. Each time we went for walks or driving around the neighborhood, whenever we saw a *stray cat* wandering around a dumpster, we always made sure he had no owner and then took him in. And, each time, we would come home to our mother with big *sweet* eyes and she just knew we were about to ask her to take in one more cat. She always said yes, even if each time she would yell, "We now have so many cats, we can't accept more, is that clear?" And then the episode repeated time and time again.

Back then we were living in the countryside of a city named Velletri, Italy.

One of our neighborhood's dumpsters was our favorite place to look for stray kitties and one day we came across tiny Polverino. He, his mother and his brothers were living behind that dumpster trying to eat the food that people were throwing in the trash.

We took home the whole family but some of Polverino's brothers died soon afterwards… we weren't able to save them. Polverino, when we took him in, seemed to be in good shape but after a few months we realized he was asthmatic and had troubles breathing. Unfortunately his life was short but everyone in the family *loved* him. The only one who lived a very long life was the mother, who died three years ago of old age. ~**LUCREZIA & LUISA** ♥

OPPOSITES ATTRACT

SCOUT & BELLA

Scout and **Bella** were in need of a loving home, so we took them in. They are schnoodles (schnauzer and poodle mix). Scout is five years old and a rambunctious, *happy* boy. He is our wild and crazy child.

Bella, 10, is laid-back and ladylike. My husband is allergic to dander so schnoodles are *perfect* for our family. We *love* them so much! ~**INGRID** ♥

My husband is allergic to dander so **schnoodles** are perfect for our family.

SCOUT   BELLA

FROM NEGLECTED TO PAMPERED

PUMPKIN, FIFI & CROOKED BEAK

Sometimes, sadly, animals are not treated well in a pet store or on a farm when they have too many animals. But luckily, little bunny **Pumpkin**, sweet duck **Fifi** and handsome **Crooked Beak** were rescued by a *loving* family and ended up in their safe and caring home.

Pumpkin came from an overcrowded pet shop, Fifi the Indian runner duck was rescued from a farm that had way too many animals. We also have her two sisters. Crooked Beak the chicken came from the same farm as well.

They are much more than barnyard pets—they are our children, Lily and Parker's, *best friends!* ~**STEPHANIE** ♥

They are **much more** than barnyard pets—they are our children, Lily and Parker's, **best friends!**

MADE FOR EACH OTHER

BERNARD

BELLA

BERNARD & BELLA

Bernard and **Bella** are fuzzy walruses, a shar-pei/cocker spaniel mix. Bernard is the older one. We adopted him after my dad died a couple years ago. He'd had mesothelioma and had suffered a stroke, so most days he struggled to communicate. But on one of the few clear days that I treasured, he told me to get the boys a dog. He thought it would be good for them and help them deal with things. He was right.

We knew as soon as we saw Bernard that we had to rescue him. And then he *rescued us*. We got healing while snuggling up with Bernard and *enjoying* this new life in our home.

Bella is the younger one. We got her about a year ago now. We specifically sought out the same breed as Bernard. We just *adore* their wrinkles. But for this adoption, we had a purpose. Our daughter was struggling with anxiety that was keeping her from sleeping. We hoped that having a dog that slept in her room would be therapeutic for her. Oddly, even though they are the same breed, they are vastly different. Bernard has longer hair and Bella is a shorthair dog. Bernard is calm and *snuggly*. Bella is playful and wiggly and silly, even as she is outgrowing her puppy phase. But, despite the fact that Bella is not the calm one, she has a calming effect on our daughter at nighttime. In fact, they seem to calm each other. Bella spends her daytime hours bouncing around the house but at bedtime she morphs into a sleepy security blanket. It's amazing how God has used these two very different dogs to bring *healing in our family!*

But the one who has benefited the most has surprisingly been our godson, Bentley. We are so blessed to share time with his parents! He spends many hours at our house and Bernard is definitely his best pal. Bentley *loves* both dogs but his buddy is Bernard. He is a fuzzy, wrinkly babysitter when I'm out of the room. Bernard watches Bentley like a mama dog with her pups. They play together and sometimes get in trouble together. They console each other and take naps together. When Bentley goes to his mom or dad's house, Bernard finds a piece of Bentley's clothing to sleep with. And when Bentley returns, Bernard brings one of his own favorite toys to the door to offer to Bentley. They are perfect for each other. ~**POLLY** ♥

IN THEIR OWN WORDS

BARNEY

BRUNO

BARNEY, BRUNO, TEDDY, LYLA & BROWNIE

"He's a pain in the neck!" Those were the words from my foster mom's mouth. I could tell my new mama did not believe her one bit! My foster mom was only being truthful. Hi, I'm **Barney**. I love lots of exercise, but I have to be very careful. I was born with hip dysplasia. Eventually, I'll need new hips. My orthopedic surgeon is super nice and thinks I'm cute. My mama says I melt her *heart*, even when I drive her nuts. She says I go in the opposite direction of the blowing wind. All that matters is that she *loves* me, and oh, how I love her... and my human baby, Nora. ~**BARNEY** ♥

Love is more than I had ever imagined.

Sometimes things are a bit cloudy in my mind. Still, I recall so much: all the salty tears I have licked off your face; the way you *smile* when I comfort you; the way you brush me; even the 100-year-old-books I chewed up when I was little! You say that I'm your soul mate. I'm trying to teach Barney to be a good soul mate to you, but he is...well, he's Barney. This dementia thing will never take away what I feel for you. I know you always say: "Who rescued who?" I say we saved each other. ~**TEDDY** ♥

My name is **Lyla**. I am a survivor, and I am *loved!* I'll never turn down beautiful flowers and tasty biscuits. Roses are my weakness, but that's not really why I pose. My humans love taking pictures of me. I love making them smile. This is far better than the gutter I was found in, starving at four weeks old. My dream is that someday all of my kind will have a warm bed, and a *loving* family like mine. ~**LYLA** ♥

They've lost count of my surgeries. I survived distemper, and I spent a long time in an incubator in the hospital. They say I'm very lucky. I think the hardships just made me *strong*. You've got to be. This world can be pretty rough. I should know: I am the boss of four big dogs. The two young ones can be a bit annoying, but they know not to get wild around me! The darn ribbon around my neck doesn't show my tough side. I wish they'd just buy me one of those spiked collars! My dad lets me be top dog. I *love* my dad more than life. ~**BROWNIE** ♥

I am swift and silent, compact yet fierce, gentle but protective. Rarely do I bark. I leave that to the rest of my pack. I am the little big dog. This family found me when I needed to be found. I had no glow in my eyes. Yet, they had hope. No life in my body, but they never gave up. This cottage is my castle. I never worry about those days when I was near death, starving and ignored for growing out of my puppy stage. Now I am here. *Love* changes things. It is a new beginning, a brighter day. It's rooting for someone when they need it most. It is belonging, and warmth. It is why I guard my family, for they guard my soul. Love is more than I had ever imagined. I do not take it for granted. ~**BRUNO** ♥

My dream is that someday all of my kind will have **a warm bed**, and a loving family like mine.

TEDDY
LYLA
NORA
BARNEY

BROWNIE

A MUTUAL RESCUE

COCO

Our sweet **Coco**, a Catahoula Mix, came to us on a rainy November day over three years ago.

My daughter-in-law, Renee, was driving home from visiting her parents. She saw something small and fuzzy in the middle of the road. The tiny, 5-weeks-old puppy was almost run over by a fast-moving truck. She stopped the car and picked up the puppy. She was cold, crying and shivering. She was out in the middle of nowhere. Someone had dumped her on the side of the road.

Renee put her in my husband, Dale's, lap and the rest is history. He named her Coco. She adores him and our whole *family loves her*.

Dale is a disabled veteran and Coco has helped him in so many ways. I think they *rescued* each other that day. ~**SALLY** ♥

PARTY ANIMALS

CUPCAKE & SPRINKLES

Cupcake is a Siamese; she is my *baby* and Lollie's best friend. She was born in my neighbors' garage and she was feral. She was so wild that we couldn't touch her. I saw her and it was *love* at first sight and her mama must have known it was meant to be because she brought her babies to me the next day. We kept Cupcake around **Sprinkles**, who was a stray kitten from another litter, and she started warming up to us. So she finally let me pick her up, started *purring* for the first time and from that point she never left my side.

One night, a stray dog attacked my cats and we couldn't find Cupcake for two days. Then a neighbor told us she was in their bushes. I stopped everything and ran to get her. She crawled out of from under the shrubs. She had a broken leg, broken toes and her tail was broken and the bone was exposed. I got an emergency vet appointment. They had to amputate her tail and put a metal rod in her leg. They were amazing and definitely saved her life. Now she's my little bobtail "bunny."

Lollie is not a rescue but it was her birthday so she celebrated with her *favorite friends*. Here they are all sharing treats: Cupcake (in the forefront), Sprinkles (the tabby in the back), and Zoey (the black and white). Lollie's friend Scout (the little Pomeranian) was a welcome guest, too. ~**ALYSSA** ♥

BFFS

ANDY

FELIX

so sweet!

ANDY & FELIX

Andy's owner was an elderly man who was forced by his son to surrender Andy and 10 other dogs to an animal shelter. Andy was supposed to be a foster and only be with us short-term. We fell in *love* with his *beautiful soul* and he became a permanent member of our family two years ago.

My 9 year-old-son, Cam, had been asking for a kitten for a long time. As it turned out, we were taking Andy to the vet for a checkup and someone had taken a sick kitten in and they were looking for a home for him. He was so little that he had no teeth and they had named him Toothless! We changed his name to **Felix** and agreed to give him a *loving*, safe and permanent home.

Cam bought everything with his own money to get ready to bring this tiny kitten home.

Andy and Felix are the *best of friends*. Andy loves his kitten so much and has unending patience with sweet but very active and playful Felix. ~**LORI** ♥

Andy and Felix are the **best of friends.**

SAVED & LOVED

HENRY, LIZZIE & COUGAR

These babies were born in my flower bed one morning in May, 10 years ago. Someone had dumped their mother in my neighborhood and, *thankfully*, she found her way to our house. She was a Siamese cat and all of her kittens were tabbies.

Sadly, one passed away in his first year. The bonded ones are **Henry** and **Lizzie** (she has white paws) and the bottom right is **Cougar**, who now lives next door with my neighbor. ~**BESS** ♥

WITH A PURE HEART

FRED & MOLLY

Fred came to me through my sister in Maryland. She has a neighbor who had trapped 17 cats in my brother-in-law's barn. I had just lost a cat and wanted to enjoy being cat-free for a while, but my sister called and told me I had to take two. So I went to look at all the kittens. It was so obvious they were related; all were either black and white, gray and white, or white and tabby.

I wanted to take another black and white because it reminded me of my last cat, Homie. My then-boyfriend prefered a gray-and-white kitten, though, because he was the friendliest. Most of the others were very feral.

FRED

I took the gray and white (soon to be Fred) and another *cutie*, his dad, Murphy, who my sister picked for me. I had never had two before. But it was fewer than my sister had; she kept all five black ones because she was fearful no one would adopt them.

Fred and Murphy were so close, always grooming each other and sleeping in a ball. Murphy unfortunately died a few years later. I was heartbroken. But Fred bounced back. He is extemely smart and very people-friendly. My roommate says he is more like a dog than cat.

Fast forward a few years when I moved into a small three-family dwelling where there were seven cats living among two of the families. One after the other, the two women who were looking after all these cats both died, and no one really wanted to care for these animals.

Very sadly, four were dumped on the street late one night, but I managed to help the remaining three before they disappeared as well.

One was Penny, a *sweet* brown tiger that I took to a no-kill shelter in Brooklyn, New York, where she got adopted in less than two weeks. Yay for one happy ending!

Then there was Sweety, a beautiful long-haired calico. She really was the sweetest cat there ever was. Even people who didn't like cats liked *this* cat. I took her in but, unfortunately, not soon

One night she jumped on the bed and I started petting her and she began **purring like crazy.**

MOLLY

after, she became sick and needed to get fluids twice every day, so I took to doing that and she lasted six months before she passed away, my little Sweety.

Lastly, there was **Molly**. About six years earlier she was a feral kitty trapped from the backyard.

When I brought her into my apartment I thought that she would just feel safe and start sleeping on my bed right away. Wrong! She was so traumatized from living the fearful life of a cat no one loved that she went under my bed and then the challenge began. She only came out to eat and ran right back under the bed.

It took two months before I started seeing a flicker of a tail as she ran back to safety, then another two months before I saw her sitting (not cowering), and then two more months before I saw her walk around. All these things are so normal but she was so fearful! It took her a long time to trust me.

Then, one night, she jumped on the bed and I started petting her and she began *purring* like crazy. I then knew we would be best buds. Today she is is still fearful of others but not of me. She will come out and sit on the couch with me in the evening, and *loves* to play. My friends can't believe I have another cat! ~**TRACY** ♥

A SHORT BUT LOVING TIME

SPANKY

About three years ago, we found **Spanky**'s photo posted online. He had been surrendered to a San Antonio, Texas, animal shelter and was 12 years old at the time.

We submitted an adoption application and, once we were approved, made the four-hour drive to pick him up. Spanky was very *calm* and immediately became *attached* to me, didn't want to leave my side and would cry when I left. I believe he was afraid that he would be abandoned again and took a few weeks to adjust to our home.

We had the pleasure and *honor* to have Spanky for two more years until he began his battle with throat cancer. He tried to stay with us as long as possible but became so ill and was suffering too much that we had to make that hard decision of letting him go. Blessed Spanky. ~**LUCY** ♥

WHEN A KISS IS MORE THAN A KISS

CHARLIE

This is the story of my little **Charlie** girl.

2015 was not our best year. We lost our rescue dog, Shifu, to cancer and then a planned move from California to Florida ended up not working out (after I'd already left a job I loved for the move) and we found ourselves unexpectedly back in California with our lives upside down. We knew we needed a dog in our life, so right after landing we visited the local rescue, Animal Friends Rescue Project in Pacific Grove, and gave them a list of all the dogs we'd seen on the website and were interested in meeting.

As soon as I was contacted, I wasted no time in setting up an appointment for the same day.

This little dog had been found wandering the streets of Salinas just a couple of months earlier. I had just one criteria for knowing if it was the right dog or not: she/he had to give *kisses*, because Shifu had been such a kissy dog and I had loved that. Charlie (then called Brownie) did this funny little crawl thing the first time we met her that *charmed* us and then she crawled right into my lap and started kissing me. I knew from that moment that she was meant for us. She must have known it too, because when we got up to head for the door, she was right there with us, thinking she was going home. We still had to fill out the paperwork at the headquarters about 20 miles away, but we made that round trip as fast as we could and picked her up that night. We changed her name from Brownie to Charlie, naming her after John Steinbeck's dog in *Travels With Charley*.

Now, almost three years later, we are a family and can't imagine not having Charlie in our lives. She makes us laugh every day as she greets each morning with enthusiasm and passion. We finally made our move to Florida and she *loves* living among lizards and squirrels, although she's not too fond of the big cranes that frequently stroll through our backyard. We take her to the beach as often as we can and she enjoys paddling in the ocean...at least for a little while. ~**JONNI** ♥

A HOME FOR LIFE

JETBOY

I was out doing my errands in February, 2011, when I came upon a dog rescue on the sidewalk with loads of animals in cages and little dog runs. It was very sad. I saw a small cage with a big black German shepherd inside with a red rope around his neck. He was back in the corner looking sad. I asked if I could walk this boy and they said yes. Once I took him for a walk around the shopping center I was hooked. He was so scared!

I walked back and was told that adoption cost $350 and they had just spayed him. I gave them a $350 check and added a $50 donation. I took **Jetboy** (named for his beautiful black coat) to the vet. He had mange and needed an update on all his shots. I waited almost three hours to get in and to get his diagnosis on his mange to see if he was okay to come and be with the other animals at our home. He needed eight weeks of pills and a booster for his shots.

We were told Jetboy had been abused. I pulled my car up at the curb and he jumped into the passenger seat. He had a *home* for life! He patrols our half acre every night and stays by my husband's chair on his big pillow and routinely sticks his paw up to daddy's chair and wants daddy to rub and talk to his paw. We allow him full access to all the other animals in our home. He is our *sweet* boy. ~**DEBBIE** ♥

Once I took him for a walk around the shopping center **I was hooked.**

ONE BY ONE

KENSIE

TROOPER

BELLA

KENSIE, TROOPER & BELLA

We lost our beloved Kayla (Monkey Face) in 2014. I noticed one day that her breathing was very labored so I took her to the vet where we found out she had aggressive cancer and a bad heart. We tried everything to save her and within two weeks sadly made the decision to let her go.

She grew up with **Kensie,** who was a year older, and he was so depressed without her here. He wouldn't eat and wanted to sleep all day. We were all pretty heartbroken so we decided to look for another little shih tzu (we *love* that breed). We looked online at pet shelters and at rescue groups but couldn't find one.

We called a lady in the area that breeds shih tzus and asked if she knew of anyone who had an older dog that we could adopt. She told us that she had a little guy that was 10 months old that a woman had to give up due to moving and asked if we wanted to come see him. We hurried over there and fell in *love* immediately. We took Kensie with us and he perked up right away and began playing with him so we took the little guy home.

He got very sick with frequent bladder infections and we thought he might have kidney disease. We finally got him healed up and all is well. We ended up naming him **Trooper** because he had been through so much.

About four months later, the woman called us to ask how he was doing and if I wanted his sister for free. I didn't even know he had a sister. We went over to see the little girl and she looked pitiful.

We were informed that she had just weaned five puppies. The woman didn't want us to put her on the floor for fear she would urinate. We took the *little girl* home and to the vet right away. The vet treated her for a urinary tract infection. We couldn't get her better so we took her to a specialist and found out she had bladder stones. They performed a procedure to get rid of them. Our poor **Bella** may have been put down if we hadn't rescued her.

All three of our pups, Trooper and Bella (4 years old) and Kensie (almost 16), light up our lives! They travel with us all the time in our vintage-inspired camper. We took a month-long road trip last year down the east coast and they were a hit wherever they went. Bella is a *beautiful* little girl and Trooper is our little clown. Having them has given a new lease on life to our little senior guy, Kensie. They *love* to go for walks every day and love to travel with us.

Pets bring us so much *joy* and *laughter* in return for a belly rub, food and shelter. They are good for our souls and bring comfort. I couldn't imagine a life without a beloved *furry* friend. ~**SANDY** ♥

Bella is a **beautiful little girl** and Trooper is our **little clown.**

BUNDLE
OF SWEETNESS

HARLEY QUINN

This is **Harley Quinn**. She is a shih tzu puppy with one brown eyes and one blue eye—and a polka dot nose!

A friend was moving away and couldn't keep this *little darling* so rather than to see her going to an unknown home, I adopted her.

She is the *light of my life* already! She won't let me out of her sight, and I love it! ~**MAUREEN** ♥

BITTERSWEET

LILLY

My first boxer, Magoo, passed away suddenly at 9 years old. I had my 2-year-old boxer, Bella, at home and it was also her second birthday. Magoo was the first dog I had as an adult by myself and I was devastated. I experienced every feeling of sadness and loss and all the "what ifs" imaginable. Yes, I had Bella still and she needed me, but I was so sad and I just wondered if I would ever truly be happy again. I know that's ridiculous, but like I said it was my first dog by myself and the first time I dealt with a

dog's serious illness and the realization that no matter how much money I was willing to spend to save or heal Magoo, sometimes there is just nothing you can do and its their time to pass on.

Eventually I decided to rescue another male boxer...for me and for Bella. I found a boxer boy online at the animal shelter and off I went on a Saturday afternoon to see him. He was emaciated and in need of a lot of patience and *love* and I knew ours was the home to do it. However the shelter told me a family had spoken for him earlier that day and he was still there because he was under the seven-day hold to see if his previous owners would claim him.

They said he was rescued with a female boxer and she was available. I really wasn't looking for a female because I had Bella and thought she would do best with another male, but I agreed to meet her. Her shelter name was Sandy. I cried when I saw her coming down the hallway. I had never seen a dog that emaciated; she was a skeleton with a boxer dog head. Her energy level was *amazing* though; she jumped all over me, but wouldn't eat any of the treats I brought. So as I got to know her in a meet-and-greet kennel, the worker came over and said she misspoke and that Sandy was spoken for also. So now both boxers I went to meet were actually spoken for and their seven-day hold would be up on Tuesday and they would go to their new homes.

I asked the worker to let me know if anything changed. Tuesday came along and the shelter called to let me know that both families were taking the dogs and they both will be going to their new homes on Wednesday. I was glad to hear that because Sandy never left my mind. I just knew she was so sick that the shelter would never be a place that she would get well. So back online I went looking for a dog. I went to work on Wednesday and around noon I received a message from the shelter saying Sandy's family decided not to get her and to call them if I was still interested. I knew a female boxer was not what I was looking for but I also knew I had to get her out of there and get her healthy and then I would find her a great family. The shelter people told me the family decided not to take Sandy because she was heartworm positive. They then explained to me that they were unable to spay her or treat her for heartworm because she was so emaciated. They would allow me to *rescue* her under the condition that I understood she might not make it. She was so sick that she would not eat.

So basically unless I could somehow get her to gain 20 pounds there was nothing more they could do for her. If I got her to gain the necessary weight they would treat the heartworm issue as well as spay her. I agreed, even though I was clueless about what I just took on. Sandy dragged me down the hallway, through two doors and out the front door of the shelter! To this day we have no idea how she knew how to get out of the shelter by the front door because she came through the back door in the animal control paddy wagon.

I knew I had to give her a lovely female name because she was *beautiful* and would one day be healthy again and look beautiful to everyone. My favorite flower is a calla lily...so I decided to name her Lilly. Well, as sick and unhealthy as she was, while I was putting my purse in the front seat of my car so I could put her in the crate, she went flying up into the front seat and *kissed* my face.

At home I had to change everything. They told me not to have her with Bella until she was a bit healthier and she also had kennel cough. Long story short: It took me six months to put 20 pounds on her because she had so many parasites, worms and the heartworms that she couldn't keep food down.

I went to bed many nights not knowing if she would be alive in the morning. I got her treated for heartworm and she was spayed. She didn't like most dogs but she loved my boxers (I forgot to mention Bella's sister had a litter of pups and Mr. Mugsy—you know the boy I was looking for— came home). So within seven months I had Lilly at 100 percent healthy. The shelter thought she was 3 years old but it was obvious when she filled out that she was an older girl with lots of gray hair, and had been overbred. She had the most *loving* personality and it was clear that someone had once loved her because she knew commands and was such a good girl.

So it was time for me to find her a family. I put a sign up at my vet's office and two weeks later I got a call from a great family. We went out to meet them and all I can say is they were a perfect couple with a young boy. They wanted to adopt her and I sat on their couch tearing up. It was then that I realized she was my dog. She was everything to me. I knew I had *fallen in love* with her and we had been through it all in the seven months to get her healthy. I couldn't let her go.

So home we went and now I had three dogs! She had saved me from my deep sadness over losing Magoo and she won my heart with her *sweet* and loving demeanor. Lilly stayed healthy for a solid year. It was a great year.

Then she developed a heart condition. She lived with heart disease for six months and I knew it was a fatal diagnosis and just a matter of time. She died next to me in bed six months after her diagnosis. It was a beautiful two years with her. From the beginning, when I didn't know if she would make it through the night, to watching her thrive, run and play, to watching her slow down and leave this earth, she was the best.

I keep a token I found in the Sundance catalog on my dresser by her picture. It reads, "Thank you for the love. You were my *angel*...now I am yours." Thank you Lilly, you are my angel. Mommy loves and misses you everyday ~**TRACY** ♥

HOPE SPRINGS ETERNAL

RILEY

One evening in December of 1989, we went "just to take a look" at a litter of puppies a friend was raising. Make no mistake, the pups were of the exact breed I had dreamed of having for years. I was raised with terrier-mix sweeties all of my childhood. This litter was wire fox terriers.

Cue the husband: "We are only going to look. We aren't home enough to have a dog." Needless to say, we returned home with a rambunctious, snuggly Christmas gift for ourselves. This wiry little imp was named **Riley**. In years to come we knew she was named correctly for the "Life of Riley" she surely had. Our Riles (her nickname) slept with us, traveled with us and walked myriad miles with us...until she couldn't. And that, unfortunately, came much too soon.

At 10 years she no longer leapt at the leash when we asked: "You want to go for a w___?" Her daily hikes were too laborious. Her magical life filled with road trips to the Pacific Northwest and east through the states of Nevada, Arizona and New Mexico were memories. Our family and neighbors at home would no longer be greeted with happy barking. All the years of antics, her strong-willed personality, her charisma and *cuddling* every evening ended on a December day. Just as the day we found our girl.

Our lives were forever *enriched* by her presence, but we have not, to my dismay, adopted another dog as the heartbreak for my husband was truly too much to bear again. Instead, we enamor ourselves with strangers on a beach and nearly anyone with a "Riley dog" so we might feel that curly tangle of fur, or garner a kiss from a sweet, long-snouted, stick-legged pup again. My heart knows that we will love another foxy again in this lifetime. ~**SHARI** ♥

LEARNING TO TRUST

FRITZ

Fritz found us November, 2011, before the snow hit! He was running the streets and ended up outside of a bronze casting shop. It took a lot of *love* and *patience* for him to trust and feel safe with us.

He is a housedog now and shares space with two found kitties we took in as his siblings! My husband named him Fritz as he thought it was an appropriate name for a German shepherd. Fritz is the greatest *joy* in our life! ~**SHARMA** ♥

LITTLE BALL OF LOVE

PARKER

Parker came to me after his human mom passed away from cancer.

I was unsure about adopting a little guy but had recently lost my 13 year-old beagle and my Labrador (I like to say he is a Labrador raised by a beagle) was ready for a new companion. So Parker came home with us and he's the part of my heart that was missing.

He's a football with legs, a chug—part Chihuahua and pug—and all personality! His *love* knows no bounds. He has been living it up traveling all over with us and then snuggling up at home. He's 11 years young and my *angel*. ~**SARAH** ♥

AS GOOD AS IT GETS

HERSHIE

HERSHIE & MINKY

I got **Hershie** about three years ago from animal care and control. I was looking for a friend for my little orange girl cat and spent a few hours a day looking at cat rescues online.

I saw Hershie—a big, chubby-cheeked ragdoll—and fell in *love* with him immediately. I visited him at the shelter, played with him, carried him around and decided to adopt him the next day. When I went to pick him up, he was gone! Someone had come by right after me and took him home. I was heartbroken. He was such a gentle, easygoing guy and also so *good looking*. I kept up my daily search and a few weeks later, lo and behold Hershie was back on the adoption page! Apparently, the person brought him back the next day saying that the cat did not like her husband.

He adapted to his new home quickly, but, unfortunately, my orange cat did not like him at all, so they just ignored each other. Hershie has always been a very gentle guy; he *loves* all people, even small children. He loves to play and often brings me leaves or hair ties to throw for him. He likes to roll in the damp tub after I shower, lie on my purse or shoes when I get home and is a kind and thoughtful companion. My *sweet* little orange cat was elderly and died about a year after bringing Hershie home. I've always rescued older cats and this was the fifth cat I'd nursed through their final illness, so I wasn't eager to go through that again soon. I decided that the next cat was going to be younger.

I was trolling craigslist looking for a needy cat and found a lady overwhelmed by pets and kids. She had three young kids, four dogs, two cats and three kittens. One of the cats got out before she could be spayed and came home pregnant. This little mama cat was a super flat-faced Persian and the babies were all black. Only one of the kittens, **Minky**, had a Persian face (but not as flat as the mom's.) I decided I had to take him. He was the *cutest cat* I'd ever seen; long fluffy coat, plume tail, chubby cheeks and the tiniest furry ears...just a darling little guy. Went I went to pick him up, the house was a little chaotic. It took a while to catch the squirmy Minky but I got him in the carrier and we drove off. The poor little fellow cried all the way home, he missed his mama! Fortunately he and Hershie became fast friends and started *playing* immediately. They chase and wrestle all the time. They are a funny pair with Hershie being more than twice Minky's size. I'm so glad I got these boys and they are so glad to have each other. ~**BRIDGET** ♥

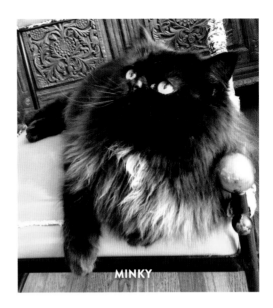

MINKY

LITTLE TREASURES

GIGI MARIE
SCARLET JOE
IVY BLEUBELLE
CAPT. DASH ROCKWELL

At 16, a friend of mine from London had a French bulldog and **I fell in love!**

GIGI MARIE, SCARLET JOE, IVY BLUEBELLE & CAPT. DASH ROCKWELL

At 16, a friend of mine from London had a French bulldog and I fell in love! At that time there were very few in the States.

Flash forward to a time when I was able to get and care for my own pets. It started with **Gigi Marie**, who looked like a guinea pig when she arrived—such a *bundle of joy* and a princess! Then came **Scarlet Joe** who is our tomboy and loves her daddy. **Ivy Bleubelle** is my partner in crime, and **Capt. Dash Rockwell** is our special needs boy.

Our "kids" are named after comic book heroes or villains! ~**STACY** ♥

PUPPY LOVE

RILEY

I drove 170 miles all the way to a town called Warner Robins, Georgia, to get **Riley**.

I pulled up to a house in the country and was led around to a shed in the backyard. Out stumbled a little half-pound *ball of fluff* that was barely able to see over the blades of grass. I scooped him up.

He was only eight weeks old and the remaining pup in the litter. It was hard to tell how long he had been away from his littermates and mother. But I didn't ask questions. It didn't matter. From the moment I laid eyes on him, I knew he was the one and we have been growing that bond ever since.

Riley has been all over the country with us—eighteen states so far. Our connection with him is unlike anything we've ever experienced with an animal.

His intelligence level is unreal. He intently listens to us when we talk and picks words he knows out of our conversations. He understands our body language and reacts to the subtlest signals.

He's 10 years old and really hasn't changed that much. He still runs like the wind, plays like a puppy and is *feisty* as can be.

We can't wait to show him the other half of the country. Here's to many more years of exploring with our best friend! **~SHEENA** ♥

LOVELY SURPRISES

OLIVE & JAX

We lost out 12-year-old shih tzu about two years ago. Our pup, Jovee, was so sad and we knew she needed a friend.

As it happened, a friend had a nephew with a friend in downtown Dallas. That friend had just *adopted* a new dog and took him on a jog when a little shih tzu found them. She had never been groomed and possibly let go after she had pups. He took her to the vet and she wasn't chipped. He placed signs and ads but no one came. He knew he couldn't afford to care for two dogs. After looking at our Facebook photos he decided that we treated our dogs like family and agreed to let us come meet her. We put Jovee in the car and headed to Dallas. Well, when we saw that little mop of a dog we knew she was ours. She was a mess! She had a little street dog in her but with *love* and training she has become the *best little dog*. **Olive** loves having her family and we love having her.

OLIVE

Jax the cat became part of our family eight years ago when I was working at a salon and a mama cat let us start feeding her. She began to *trust* me. So the day she delivered her kittens, my coworker Chuck helped me put her and her babies in a box in my car. I called my husband and said: "Guess what? We are having babies!" Within weeks, I put their pictures on Facebook and friends all chose a kitten. We found mama cat a nice home on a farm in the county and we *fell in love* with baby Jax and kept him.

He rules our home and he lets us *share* it with him!
~MISTEY ♥

JAX

We found mama cat a nice home on a **farm in the county** and **we fell in love with baby Jax** and kept him.

NEVER APART

CLEOPATRA, COTTON & GUSS

I have always been a bunny *lover* from the time I was a young girl and was surprised on my 8th birthday with my first pet rabbit. For most of my adult life, I have enjoyed house rabbits as pets. When my 6-year-old mini Holland lop, Gucci, who I *adopted* from the House Rabbit Society, died from cancer a few years ago, I longed for another bun. During my search I found a tiny Netherland Dwarf Hotot (pronounced "Hoe Toe"), who, with her sister, a blue-eyed white Netherland Dwarf, were headed for the Georgia National Fair.

When I was introduced to this petite snow-white bunny I knew immediately that I wanted to keep her. I was told that she was not "perfect" enough for breeding or showing and that she was the runt of the litter. I also found out that she and her sister *bunny*, who was at her side at the time of our first meeting, had never been apart. What was I to do? How could I separate these sister bunnies? I couldn't. I took both of them and aptly named the tiny Hotot **Cleopatra** for her beautiful eyes and gave the name **Cotton** to the blue-eyed, soft-as-cotton white fur ball.

It is obvious that Cleopatra was the runt of the litter—she is such a clumsy little creature. She frequently stumbles and ends up on her back and cannot turn over so often that our dog, Guss, barks in the middle of the night so that we know she is in distress and needs help. He is especially fond of her.

CLEOPATRA

These silly rabbits still are never apart, constantly grooming each other, *snuggling*, and pushing each other around in their hutch to grab the best bite of freshly grown basil or lettuce. Occasionally they play dress up and do photo shoots with me, depending upon their mood and the holiday. They bring us

I have always been a
bunny lover from the time
I was a young girl.

COTTON

joy and we are happy that we saved them from not only being separated but also from living in small cages and doing fair tours until they were sold.

When we decided that our young son was old enough to enjoy and take care of a dog in addition to our then house rabbit, Gucci, we began the search. With Gucci in mind, we had to be attentive to the particular breed and size of a new dog; we did not want a dog that was not fond of rabbits! One late summer night, I saw a photo of a black-and-white King Charles cavalier/poodle mix, a cavapoo, on the Petfinder website. The picture of this puppy not only reminded me of my childhood dog, but also had the exact birth date as our son. It was a no-brainer and I woke my husband up that night and told him that I found our dog.

He was bred to be a show dog and because his markings were not symmetrical, the breeder put him up for adoption when he was about a year old. When we drove through the country roads of rural Georgia to meet him for the first time, what we found was a scraggly looking mess of a mutt, but we could not resist him. A week later we adopted **Guss** (his name at the time, which we kept); we call him our $2,000 rescue dog. He was infested with fleas, ear mites, heartworms and his fur was matted, but he had a tail that never stopped wagging. For a long time, he was fearful of deep male voices and we still are not sure why.

GUSS

Today he is the most loyal, *affectionate*, and obedient dog and we could not imagine our home without him. He loves to chase squirrels and chipmunks in our yard, never leaves my side while I am working from home, is a faithful companion to our son, wakes us up on the weekends so he can go on a walk with my husband (whose deep voice he loves now), and looks after Cleopatra and Cotton. **~SUZANNE** ♥

INSEPARABLE

NASH

PAXTON

NASH & PAXTON

We *rescued* **Nash** from a single man who didn't have enough time to spend with his pup. After going through Nash's vet records we realized we were his fifth owners in his short 7-year life. He came with some aggression issues and this was expected with all the changes he had to endure. I actually returned him once to his previous owner. I cried the whole way home and talked it over with my husband. I called later that night to ask if I could come back the next day to get Nash back. After many hours of working with him and re-training him, and many emails consulting with a specialist at UC Davis vet school, I am *happy* to say that Nash is a valued member of our family. He has his forever home with us.

We adopted **Paxton** from a lady who had a litter of unregistered boxer pups. He was the last of the litter and only 7 pounds of *love* when we got him. He is now a lap dog. He is my shadow and follows we everywhere. He doesn't have one aggressive bone in his body. Paxton has accepted Nash as his new little brother and the two have grown quite *fond* of each other. They are *inseparable* and love to *play* and run in the backyard chasing squirrels. They enjoy sunbathing, camping and long walks on the beach. ~**DEDE** ♥

They are inseparable and **love to play** and run in the backyard chasing squirrels.

THE ASSISTANTS

PEACHIE

O'MALLEY & LULU

PEACHY, LULU AND O'MALLEY

Peachie, **LuLu** and **O'Malley** do what they can to help me in the office. Mostly they inspire me to take naps! I also spend a lot of time pulling cat hair out of my folders...

Peachie disappeared for a year. She ended up about a hundred miles away, over a mountain. She had been going to the back door of someone who would feed her and then she would take off back into the woods.

One day she came to the back door limping and all beaten up, so the homeowner took her to a vet who scanned her and found a chip. That's how I got her back.

I drove late into the night to go get her and when I got there the doctor showed me to her cage and she looked at me and said, "Meow meow meow *meow* meow!"

I asked the doc if she could possibly remember me after all that time and he said she must because the whole time she was there she hadn't said one word to him!

Lulu and Peachie were both *rescued* from the West Los Angeles Animal Shelter.

O'Malley belonged to my housekeeper's daughter while she was at college. When she and her roommates graduated, no one could take him. So I took him in. ~**SUNDAY** ♥

CHANGE OF HEART

WYNN

Nine years ago my husband and I had to put down our *beloved* 17-year-old rescue cat named Buzzy. He was like a son to us, as we don't have any children. We were devastated. Our home was so empty without our precious baby. My husband desperately wanted to rescue another kitty but I just wasn't ready. My heart was so broken, but to appease my husband, I finally agreed to look for another *kitty* even though we could never replace our Buzzy. We searched many shelters throughout New England, spending countless hours and weekends traveling and meeting with so many wonderful kitties. When I would first meet potential kitties to adopt, I would greet them with "Hi, what's your name?"

One day while browsing on the Internet, we came across a longhair black-and-white Persian mix that looked really *cute*. His name was Hadji. The next weekend, we drove to the shelter to see him, which was about an hour's drive from us. Upon meeting him, we found that he had a big personality, and he came over to me and started licking my toes as I was wearing flip flops.

I thought that it was a sign that he liked me! Still, I had that uncertainty about allowing another kitty into my broken heart. So, we left the shelter without him.

The following week went by slowly as my husband and I kept thinking about Hadji, and wondering if we had made a mistake. We went back to the shelter's website and found out that he was no longer there. We were very disappointed and upset, and regretted not adopting him when we had the chance.

With low expectations, we called the shelter to see if there was a chance that he was still available. We held on while they checked, and learned he was transferred to another location for highly adoptable cats. He was still available! Thank God! We were so relieved! We told them we would come immediately to adopt Hadji, as we knew we had finally found the one.

We changed his name from Hadji to **Wynn**. Do you know what "Wynn" stands for? Well, do you remember earlier in our story I mentioned that when we met kitties I would always greet them with "What's your name"? Well "Wynn" is an acronym and stands for that. Along with our *beloved* Buzzy, Wynn is the best kitty we could have ever asked for! ~**ANN** ♥

A WAY OF WORKING OUT

CALI

My husband, Mark, was volunteering at NKLA (a no-kill shelter) during the summer of 2016, when he saw **Cali**, a 1-year-old pointer mix who stood out in a sea of pit bulls and Chihuahuas.

We had previously owned English pointers and were ready to *rescue* another. But there was Clarissa, waiting for us to take her away. The name did not suit her tomboy attitude, so we used some of the letters and called her "Cali," short for California where we had recently moved to from New York.

Mark and I felt guilty that we had not *adopted* a special needs or older dog, but, eight months later, Cali developed epilepsy. We got exactly the dog we were looking for. ~**VICKI** ♥

MAKING NEW FRIENDS

SABRINA, TIGER & RAMBO

We adopted **Sabrina** from the Mary S. Roberts Rescue in Riverside, California, way back in 2002 after our kitty Katie passed away. At the time, we also had a German shepherd named Xena the Warrior Princess and she and Sabrina were *best* buddies. We then *adopted* **Rambo** from Coastal German Shepherd Rescue in Southern California in 2009, after I retired.

We also *fostered* kittens from Mary S. Roberts and received **Tiger Lily** when she was only 3 weeks old and raised her. My husband had back surgery and fell in *love* with Tiger when she would sleep beside him while he was recuperating. He couldn't part with her so we adopted her back in 2011. Rambo loves to boss Tiger around and sometimes she has had enough and will chase him around, hissing at him and trying to scratch him, and he will run and hide behind me! ~**JENNY** ♥

SABRINA

TIGER LILY, RAMBO & SABRINA

My husband had back surgery and **fell in love with Tiger** when she would sleep beside him while he was recuperating.

HEAVEN SENT

MIK

The saying goes, "all dogs go to heaven," but I like to imagine that they are also sent from heaven.

I started volunteering at a local animal shelter in my town, where I would drop off supplies and walk the dogs and play with them.

My husband has been allergic to dogs for years, so this was the only way I could give back and selfishly *cuddle* with all of the dogs. On a warm day in May, I went by the shelter to see which dogs could use a walk and the young man working there pointed at Mik's crate. "Mik was rescued from an abusive home in Texas and has since been returned twice to the shelter because his fur is so coarse and he sheds. He is currently our most docile dog here." From the minute I saw Mik's sad eyes, I knew I had to take him *home*. He was only two years old, and any time a person approached him or tried to pet him he would flop over and flinch. It broke my heart.

Without even consulting with my husband, I adopted him.

What happened next still to this day baffles me.

My husband, who is an animal lover at *heart*, gave Mik a chance, and, somehow, he didn't start sneezing or develop hives or anything—he had no allergic reaction at all! We like to think that it is Mik's coarse fur that makes him unique and a perfect fit for our family. Mik *loves* to howl, play catch and he is such a good sport when my daughter comes over to dress him up and take his pictures. Mik is our furry son and his lovable personality brings so much *joy* to our lives. Above all of that, he has a great smile! ~ELISA ♥

SELFLESSNESS, DEDICATION & LOVE

SCOOTER & EINSTEIN

This is the story of two little dogs deemed "unadoptable" due to their severe disabilities and how a selfless, dedicated and caring woman rescued them and proved that love heals all.

SCOOTER'S STORY

One little paralyzed dog changed the course of one human's life and went on to save other handicapped dogs!

I already had a little bichon frise named FiFi when I decided that she needed a *friend*. I searched all the local shelters but to no avail. So I went online to find a rescue. Don't know how it happened, but I came across a video of this little black poodle mix dog. He was very skinny with long, ragged hair, dragging his little body along the grass. My heart just broke for him. This was in December, 2006, and I had never really thought about a dog being disabled! I'd never seen one! Where did they all go? I don't know why but I found myself watching this video almost every single day for three weeks and each time I cried uncontrollably for him and how helpless and alone he must feel. Nobody wanted a dog that was born paralyzed, with a hump on his back, twisted back legs and a heart problem. He also needed to have his bladder expressed every four hours and at least once during the night and wear a diaper, like a newborn baby.

By now 1,189 people had viewed the video, and I decided that I needed to *save him*. I was the *only* applicant. Within three weeks he was transferred up from the South with his little wheelchair! I had never expressed a bladder before, but I was told I could learn on YouTube. It wasn't that easy. He also had pneumonia and suffered from terrible constipation because he refused to drink water because he had suffered from a lifetime of very painful bladder infections.

Bit by bit, I addressed each of his issues and he just *flourished!* For almost five years, every time when I expressed his bladder and put on a clean diaper, he would look up at me with those huge brown eyes and lick my face, as if to say thank you!

He loved everyone and everyone who met him loved him. He was especially loved by his terrified foster sister, Lilly, who had been rescued from an illegal puppy mill (video online on YouTube) in Warren, Tennessee, through Paws New England. She had 10 pounds of matted fur on her when found, was emaciated beyond belief, blind in one eye and suffered from extreme PTSD. She had never been outside, seen daylight or touched grass. Bit by bit, she trusted Scooter and he really brought her out of her shell. He gave her the confidence she didn't have, and she was his protector from any danger. They *adored* each other. I of course couldn't separate them, and ended up adopting her too. I know without a doubt that she would never have blossomed without his help. Scooter saved her too.

Everyone was drawn to Scooter. He was *sweet*, loving, funny, and, above all, everyone who met him said they felt something very spiritual around him. He was the baby that I had never had, and I was the mommy that he had never had. He died suddenly on October 13, 2013.

Scooter changed the course of my life. When he died, I vowed that I would continue to rescue the most severely and unadoptable disabled dogs that no one wanted. In the last 10 years, as well as still having FiFi, I have gone on to adopt Lilly, Einstein, Teddi and Trixie, as well as three cats. As the disabled dogs pass on, I adopt another one in Scooter's honor.

EINSTEIN'S STORY

Einstein's story is of the most extreme abuse. And how he overcame his disabilities and fears and still never gives up is incomprehensible! Einstein was found in late 2012 wandering the streets of Los Angeles, alone and starving. No one knows how long he had been there by himself but he was very old, frightened and in extreme pain, with raw bones on all legs and feet and cuts up to his elbows! He was taken to an animal shelter where he only weighed 7 pounds and was in such bad condition they decided to euthanize him. His life was saved by a rescue that scooped him up from an untimely death!

Einstein had been dumped at the side of the road from an illegal puppy mill. He had been forced to stand on chicken wire in a cage for his entire life. He no longer had feet or pads on them. He was down to the bone on all four paws. His back legs were probably broken at one time, and had grown upwards to almost look like an elbow. He also had most of both ears missing. There was hair missing from one side of his face and a huge cut on the other that would not heal, and a piece of his mouth missing. The rescue group was wonderful and paid for numerous surgeries on his feet. He needed 24-hour care. He had to have his feet cleaned, medicated and wrapped in bandages every day. But, he was still was determined to walk, if only just for a few steps. Once again, no one would adopt him because of the severity of his disabilities. The rescue flew him from LA to me in February, 2013. He

arrived in very frail condition. He was terribly thin and still had open wounds on all four legs.

Things were to get much, much worse. Einstein wouldn't eat much and soon his diarrhea turned into bleeding colitis. It was uncontrollable and now he wouldn't even drink water! Also, his feet were not healing at all and now the skin from both ears had fallen off and couldn't be reattached. From head to foot, he was bleeding with open wounds. After about fifteen office visits, multiple medications and prescription food, the vet insisted he be euthanized. She said that he was very old and had had four great months out of the puppy mill and we should be happy. I felt sick to the pit of my stomach that after a lifetime of abuse, he was going to be thrown away so easily! I refused to euthanize him. I told her that he needed 4 good years after the puppy mill, and I was determined to give them to him!

Two days later, I went to another vet. We both agreed that he was in very bad shape, but not terminal. Bit by bit, he and I dealt with one issue at a time. Einstein went on steroids to help his feet, ears and mouth heal. His diet was changed and he was given antibiotics, which eventually controlled the bleeding colitis. He was also diagnosed with stage 4 heart disease. Later he was treated for allergies, which, as it turned out, is why he scratched the skin off both ears and rubbed his nose practically off! He also was diagnosed with advanced eye disease. His right eye was extended and would not shut, so he would look dead while he was sleeping. But Einstein has been treated daily to keep his feet, ears and nose healed and healthy. His colitis is controlled with prescription food and medication. He gets daily drops for his eye and medicine for his allergies. Unfortunately, he had to be removed from the steroids recently because his heart disease has worsened and he has since developed COPD.

In February, 2017, we celebrated his **four years of freedom**. It was one of the happiest days of my life! I promised him those and it was my honor to give them to him! He deserved it so much!

In December of 2016, I was told he would probably not live through Christmas or the New Year. But, here it is 2018 and he's still going! Everyone says that he doesn't want to die, because this is the only *happiness* he has ever known, and he knows he is *loved!* He is now taking about 16 medications a day, but he won't give up. He is also one of the happiest dogs that I have ever known. He *loves* his life, his homemade dinners and treats. He is most excited when we all go for a drive in the car or walks in his stroller. He is still very alert and watches everything around him and loves to sniff the air! He also loves luxury, and I am constantly fluffing up his pure down comforter on his bed. He is loved beyond belief! And I think he has a story to tell about determination and forgiveness. ~**YVONNE** ♥

FROM TRASH TO TREASURE!

MISSY

This is our **Missy**. 12 years ago I found this little girl in a dumpster. I believe we found each other and she steals my *heart* more everyday.

We now have four rescues, including Missy, and we *love* them all so much! ~**SHARON** ♥

THE GUARDIAN

OLLIE

This is my **Ollie**. He is a shih tzu, and a *sweet*, loving little man. He walks very politely on his leash and loves veggies and fresh foraging in the summer!

He came to me as a foster puppy nine years ago and, of course, I had to *adopt* him! AC Paw, a local rescue organization, had taken him in. He had a health issue and needed to be on medication for the rest of his life and his mom could not afford the cost.

Ollie is our guard dog. He protects his home, his mom and dad and his little brother, Bailey, (also a shih tzu) with *passion*. He takes his job very seriously.

He has a lot of anxiety when traveling in a car or when people he is not familiar with approach him. I try to help him overcome his fears with a soothing voice, lavender spray and *lots of love*. **~TERI** ♥

Ollie is our guard dog. He protects his home.
He takes his job **very seriously.**

PAIN REMEDY

RACHEL & ALEX

On the same day my mother passed away, my husband greeted me at the door and told me to sit down. My first thought was, "What could he possibly tell me that could be as bad as losing my mother?" He then told me that my 15-year-old cat and constant companion, Alley, had died while I was taking care of my mom.

Up to that point I had kept myself together, but I finally crumpled in a pile of tears and broken heart.

Anyone who knows me well knows, though I love dogs, I am a *cat person*. I have often said that I would not live a day without a cat.

My dear husband called me the next day and said the local humane society was having an event in town. There was only one cage left. A small grey-and-white kitten crawled out of a cardboard box in the corner. I picked her up and she purred like she was home!

Then another kitten crawled out of the box... Oh no, they were sisters! The second one snuggled up to my husband and then he said the 5 *sweetest* words: "Do you want them both?"

Though my heart still aches as I miss my mom and Alley, these *precious*, smart, *loving* little kittens have given me a reason to smile each and every day. ~**VALARIE** ♥

NEW FRIENDSHIPS

ROCKET

HAILEY

PEANUT

ROCKET, HAILEY & PEANUT

We had been searching for a year for a new dog after my 13-year-old beloved golden retriever passed away. One day, we walked into a pet store to look at retrievers for adoption and there was this tiny little Pomeranian with a white heart on his forehead! It was Valentine's Day, too! We fell in *love*, and Rocket has been a companion to me every day since (10 years)!

We also found Hailey, a *sweet* Merle Pomeranian for my daughter, Aimee, who works at a pet hospital and loves animals.

We also have three hutches for seven bunnies, including Peanut! ~**VICKIE LYNN** ♥

SHORT & SWEET

SUGAR

We rescued our sweet little Yorkie **Sugar** from a high-kill shelter in Tennessee. She is the *love* of our lives. ~**JOANNE** ♥

ACTS OF KINDNESS

MUDDY

MUDDY

My wife was speaking with a pet rescue network about a cat that was in need and on the list to be euthanized. I got there, and he was huge—the biggest cat I have ever seen; not the fattest (though I do call him "fat boy") but so long, and tall.

He came home and was very afraid. We had two cats and a dog, and they were all getting along fine, but it was a lot for him. Within a week, he developed an illness that nearly killed him. He had a type of infection from the kennel, plus stress from the whole process, that had his eyes covered with mucous. It was horrifying. The vets inserted a tube into his stomach that we had to feed him through; it was very difficult.

Somehow, he got well and has been a *sweet boy*. **Muddy** doesn't quite give back the same way many animals do, and he keeps mostly to himself. Still, he is largely very sweet and *loves* to eat and sleep and play with his toys.

ENO

ENO

Eno is a tiny bundle of *sweetness*. Someone was walking him down our block saying, "Sorry I have to take you to the shelter, buddy…" which we overheard. Right away, he was taken in by us! He had bare patches where his skin nearly showed through but was so *cute*. Our vet loved him and said, "This is the best dog you have ever brought me." His coat healed up very quickly and he is a *beautiful* little dog. He is so sweet and adorable and heart-stealing, constantly.

TOM

Tom the beagle was being returned to a local NYC shelter, Social Tees, where my wife spotted his incredible *cuteness* and presence. He had been in several foster homes, but no one could deal with him. He was a special needs dog. Our vet felt he had been overcome with heat stroke to the point of brain damage, perhaps long ago. He had been found wandering a country road somewhere in Tennessee. Somehow, through rescue networks, he wound up in the East Village of Manhattan, where we took him in.

Tom could not respond to his name, or anything, really. He would wander and just stare into space. He loved to eat. He liked to be petted but also would pull away sometimes. He was always sweet. He had an inherent sweetness that was undeniable. I had no idea how many people love beagles. Walking him meant saying hello to a lot of people who had to say, "I *love* your beagle." He was really beautiful. He did not have a mean bone in his body.

TOM

Over time, he weakened. Caring for Tom those years had a lot of meaning, despite being so much work. Though he was so utterly out of it, I felt he was very *grateful* for his life, his orthopedic bed and the food he ate, after who knows what his existence was in the back roads of the South. Tom's rescue was a true testament to the notion that anyone can be saved, even an old hound who could barely do a single normal, doggish thing.

LUNA

LUNA

Luna was in a shelter in upstate New York, near where we were living in the country at the time. The shelter person pointed to the cage and she said she was in there. But there was no animal to be seen. She was underneath a piece of fabric, and they said she did that a lot. She seemed so scared! We just had to take her home.

Luna and Muddy don't get along very well, but they have managed over the years. She is *loving*, for the most part, and very beautiful; every hair on her body seemingly is pure white. She still likes to go under things, as well as to up-high places wherever she can find them. She is quite *playful*. She has a sensitive spot on her back, so she lays on my chest and I gently massage her spine, which, after years with us, she not only tolerates but now *loves*—she comes to me for it. Like all our rescues over the years, Luna has seemed very *happy* to have been taken out of the shelter where she likely would have perished. ~**BRIAN** ♥

A GOOD SAMARITAN

LULU

My neighbor, a bus driver, rescued **Lulu** and her litter from a city bus yard. She also had all of them fixed and gave me one of the kittens.

She took the others to a pet adoption clinic. They all found homes. How *kind* of her to have saved these babies!

Lulu has brought me much *love and joy*. She is 12. ~**TESS** ♥

LUCKY DOGS (AND CAT)!

"When the Man waked up he said, 'What is Wild Dog doing here?' And the Woman said, 'His name is not Wild Dog any more, but the First Friend, because he will be our friend for always and always and always.'"—Rudyard Kipling, *The Jungle Book*

ASPEN

ASPEN, HADLEY, DUDLEY, RAVEN...AND SYLVESTER

Aspen, **Hadley** and **Raven** are Australian shepherds. "Aspen Colorado" was Aspen's official name; it fit her because of her beautiful colors and it reminded me of the snow and nature. Hadley was small when we first got him and I wanted to give him a big name that suited his personality.

12-year old Raven is my oldest dog. Her name came about because of her colors, which reminded me of the raven bird. She is our *sweet girl* and loves everyone. We did paper routes at night and she *loved* going in the car and sitting on the papers.

Mr. Dudley is a Great Pyrenees and 150 pounds of *pure love*. He thinks he is a lap dog. He is 5 years old. We have a love of big gentle giants. His name came about because of his clumsiness! **Sylvester,** aka Mr. Personality, was a stray that adopted us. We *love* them so! ~**VANESSA** ♥

HADLEY

RAVEN

We have a love of **big gentle giants.**

DUDLEY

SYLVESTER

TWICE AS NICE

CINDERELLA & MONA

Three years ago, we rescued **Cinderella** from a horrible situation. She was supposedly 13 but we think she was 10. She was owned by a young married couple that went on to have two precious little boys who loved her so much. They would squish their tiny faces into hers in *delight*.

But the couple got divorced and the mother of the two boys neglected Cinderella sometimes for days at a time as she was trying to sell her house and move into an apartment. As the woman struggled just to keep her boys she decided to train pit bull puppies and got two or three of them. My daughter watched poor Cinder get kicked down the stairs and pushed aside, sometimes only eating leftovers off the little boys plates.

When the woman decided to move across the country, she didn't want to take *sweet* Cinderella.

My daughter knew that at her age no one would *adopt* her. So, five days before Christmas, my husband and I said, "Bring her here!" How could we not?! She is our princess and sleeps on the down chaise every night!

We call **Mona** our sobriety pup. My daughter was struggling with addiction and I thought a puppy might help. (Of course that was just silly...or was it?) Mona is going on 8 ½ and my daughter is 8 years sober! So it's clear that Mona's *rescue* worked both ways! ~**CAREY** ♥

SOMETHING TO CROW ABOUT

CAROL

I received a call about an abandoned farm to go visit for junking.

When we got there, it looked like someone had been renting a little house on the property, decided to have chickens only to leave them to starve or freeze. We quickly wrapped them all up and raced home to try to save them.

Too fragile and weak, most died. **Carol** the rooster was insanely protective of the others and clearly mourned the loss of his little family.

He nearly died himself but managed to survive. He now follows us like a puppy. Being non-typical for a pet, he is a reminder that all animals deserve to be *loved* and saved and will certainly *love* us back. Welcome home to my farm, Carol. I promise I will love you forever. ~**CELESTE** ♥

I also have six dogs, one cat, two ducks, a peacock, an adopted baby moose and 32 chickens!

SAYING GOODBYE

TEX

We rescued **Tex** from the shelter in our town. He came in like a lion and out like a lamb.

When we first brought him home, he was crazy, hyper and all he wanted to do was to fetch balls. I asked my husband if we could take him back but he said, "No, just let me work with him."

Fast forward to nine years later. At the age of 12, we lost our *sweet* spirited Tex to cancer. We never even knew he was sick. He was everywhere I was and became my best friend.

He left silently and took a large part of my *heart* with him. I will miss him forever but am so glad I had the chance to experience such a blessing disguised in brown fur, soft velvety ears and a *heart of gold*. ~**YVONNE** ♥

He was everywhere I was and became my **best friend.**

PET PORTRAITS

Expressing love for animals comes in many ways but, for some, art is the answer. With charcoal, pencil, ink, watercolor and hand-stitched portraits, these three artists celebrate the endearing spirit and personality of beloved pets past and present. They not only capture their physical appearance, but also their unique essence.

"Our pets are an extension of us. I love painting your beloved friends. We are blessed with them for only a short time. Remembering their essence is so peaceful and brings joy with every view." ~ **Lizzi**

Lizzi can be reached at: *lesfleurs11@hotmail.com*

> "One of my favorite endeavors is to draw 8" x 10" ink and watercolor furbaby portraits for yourself or a loved one. This is a heartfelt gift that I find often turns out to be a remembrance of a love now in heaven. **~Debbie**

To contact Debbie email: *debbie@mypatchofbluesky.com*

Georgia

Miss Georgia chose my husband, Jim, to be her new servant while we were visiting the Palm Springs (no-kill) Animal Shelter. She was sitting on the very top of a tall cat tree and patted Jim on his head as he walked by. He sat down in a chair and she came and sat on his lap. Georgia had been in the shelter for six months, which was surprising to us as she is very social. She was already spayed when she arrived at the shelter, so clearly had been someone's pet before. Jim called her Georgia after the artist Georgia O'Keefe because of her unusual markings. Her shelter name was Ginger (because of her ears) so she easily adapted to the new name. She is an insanely loving cat, adores being cuddled, lying on laps and meeting new people, demanding that they make a fuss of her. –**Melissa**

Sunflowers

It had been almost a year since our dog Abby had died, and Marcia thought it was time to begin looking for another pup.

"Now, kids," she warned, "we're just looking today. We want to take our time and find the perfect dog." So the four of us (me, Marcia, Riley and Kate) set off for the Guilford County Animal Shelter that Saturday. An hour or so later, the five of us—me, Marcia, Riley, Kate and Sunflower— were heading home.

Sunflower had the pull on us. Still does. –**The Bell family**

Magoo

 My cat Magoo was rescued from a shelter in Newport, RI. He was scraggly, scarred, diabetic and completely overlooked. As soon as I saw him, he captured my heart. He lived to be 17 years young, was featured on NBC News with Brian Williams for his commentary about killing birds (Magoo was a pacifist and never bothered his feathered friends while outside on the patio), and never met a squirrel he didn't love. Now he rests under his favorite hydrangea bush and forever in my heart. —**Nancy**

Sofie

⌃ Sofie is my 13-year-old Pekeapoo (Pekinese/ toy poodle mix), and I've had her since she was a tiny 3-pound puppy. She's smart, funny, obstinate and a great little companion and friend. I love her to bits and feel blessed to have her in my life. She's now living with me in Stratford-upon-Avon, in the UK, and goes for walks along the banks of the River Avon and through the grounds of Holy Trinity Church, where Shakespeare is buried, every day. —**Barbara**

Jed

Jed loved Neil, the man who rescued him from a newspaper parking lot, best. He tolerated the rest of the family. He was an old soul who survived bone cancer, walking without complaint on three legs for the last several years of his life. Turn ons: belly rubs and sunshine. Turnoffs: children. He lived to be 19 years old and is missed. But he is never far away; we had him cremated, and he sits on our bookshelf. —**Millie**

Oscar

My Yorkshire terrier, Oscar, was the epitome of the phrase "man's best friend." Many times we form special bonds with our furry companions that seem to span all time and space. We were always connected no matter how far away we were in actuality, and I still think of and talk to him daily. He was adored by so many and I am blessed beyond words to have amazing memories, photographs and artwork of my very best friend. –**Matthew**

Haboobie

Anna commissioned Haboobie's portrait for a foster mom who has fostered 53 fur babies in Madison, Alabama.

Haboobie was a tiny, pitiful rescue. He was mistaken for a girl for the first few weeks but his mom got that all sorted out. He's now happily settled in Alabama with a foster sister named Beener and nobody calls him "little" these days!

Lucy

Lucy is a 5½ year old German shepherd/pit bull mix rescued from Peoria County Animal Protective Services (PCAPS) on March 18, 2014. She was significantly underweight and malnourished when she was surrendered to the shelter. I didn't have a very clear picture of her background when I first adopted her, but she was so timid that she would hardly let anyone near her. Now she seldom leaves my side and is healthy and happy! –**Kyle**

"Embroidery takes a lot of patience and accuracy, especially when it's done by hand, not machine. I find cross-stitching to be very relaxing, therapeutic and rewarding. Pet lovers say that my renditions done from photos are nothing short of mirror image." ~ **Sylvie**

For information, email Sylvie at: *shappy@wandoo.fr*

Rue

Gracie

Riley

Love of animals is a universal impulse, a common ground on which all of us may meet. By loving and understanding animals, perhaps we humans shall come to understand each other. —LOUIS J. CAMUTI, "The Cat Doctor"

#fifianimalrescues